MEET ME AT THE CHÂTEAU

A 1912 advertisement for the
luxurious new Château Laurier Hotel.

Meet me at the CHÂTEAU

A Legacy of Memory / Joan E. Rankin

Natural Heritage Books

Toronto

Permissions

Recollections of People, Press and Politics. Gratton O'Leary, copyright 1977, Macmillan of Canada.
The Long Run. Jack Cahill, The Canadian Publishers, McClelland and Stewart Limited.
A History of the Canadian National Railway. G.R. Stevens, MacMillan Publishers, 1973 (Mrs. G.R. Stevens).
"The New Château Laurier, Ottawa", *The Journal*. Nov. 1930, The Royal Architectural Society of Canada.
National Archives of Canada, Record Group 30, Vol. 12673, Items 1347; Vol. 12613, Item 441; Vol. 12634, Items 711, 712; Vol. 12644, Item 888; Vol. 12638, Item 763; Vol. 12673, Item 1331.

Every effort has been made by the author to obtain permission for all material reproduced in this book. If any omissions have occurred, corrections will be made in future reprints.

The author gratefully acknowledges the support of the Ontario Arts Council

Canadian Cataloguing in Publication Data
Rankin, Joan E.
    Meet me at the Château
Includes bibliographical references and index.
ISBN 0-920474-62-4

1. Château Laurier (Ottawa, Ont.) - History.
2. Ottawa (Ont.) - Social life and customs. I. Title
TX941.C43R3 1990   647.94713'8401   C90-095702-6

Design: Steve Eby

Printed and bound in Canada by Hignell Printing Limited

For my husband, Willie
our children, Mary, Bill, Eileen, Cathy
and all my grandchildren —
a legacy of memory.

THE AUTHOR

Born at King's Lynn, Norfolk, England, Joan (Keogh) Rankin was but four months old when in September, 1919, she arrived in Canada with her parents. The family settled in Ottawa and Joan in time attended St. Mary's Separate School, Immaculata High School, Glebe Collegiate Institute and Ottawa High School of Commerce.

For nine most enjoyable years (July 1943 to April 1952), Joan worked as a Trans-Canada Airlines passenger agent in the lobby of the Château Laurier Hotel. Over the ensuing years, her enthusiastic appreciation of the hotel stayed with her.

Six years of fact-finding interviews and writing has ultimately resulted in her published tribute to the Château.

With her husband William J. Rankin, a retired career army officer, they are the parents of four adult children. Hobbies include reading, volunteer work, flower arranging and travel.

The Chateau Laurier
showing new wing addition
Ottawa, Canada

Chateau Laurier
Ottawa.

CONTENTS

ACKNOWLEDGEMENTS

I wish to express my grateful thanks to all those kind people who assisted me in any way. My editor Elizabeth Lancaster and typist Corry Sleegers were both indispensable. J. Norman Lowe, retired C.N. History Officer and Glenn T. Wright, Archivist, National Archives of Canada, have helped immensely, also the Royal Architectural Institute of Canada.

Former and present Château Laurier employees, families and countless friends of the Château cooperated to make this project possible.

I acknowledge, also, the assistance of the May Court Club of Ottawa; the Rotary Club of Ottawa; Mrs. Alexandra Fitzerald, W.C. Heine, retired Editor of the *London Free Press*; Mr. Doug Small, Ottawa Bureau Chief, Global Television; The Parliamentary Library, Notman Photographic Archives; McCord Museum, Montreal; Mrs. Mary Monteith, Stratford, Ontario; Mr. George Tassé, Ottawa; Ms. Connie Romani, C.N.R. Customer Service Montreal; Mr. Patrick Watson, Chairman, CBC; Mr. Bill Kehoe, Radio Noon, CBO Ottawa; Mr. Terry Campbell, CBC FM Toronto; Robert F. Hyndman, Ottawa; Mr. Gerry Arial, Silver Rose Florist, Ottawa; Mr. Andy Andrews, Ottawa, Andrews-Newton Photographers; Senator Keith Davey, Ottawa; Mr. J. Ross Tolmie, Q.C., Ottawa; Mr. Robert Bryce, retired Deputy Minister of Finance; Mr. Lloyd Chisamore, retired; Mrs. Carol Morrissey, editing; S. Jeanne Mainville, R.C. Diocesan Centre, Ottawa. Anne Lodge, now retired Public Relations Director, Sandi Digras, Public Relations Director, and Gloria Manson, Executive Assistant to Mr. Peter Howard, General Manager, made it posible for me to wander around the hotel at will. They also invited me to the Press Breakfast on the occasion of the opening of the first phase of reconstruction in 1985 and to the Seventy-Fifth Anniversary Party, June 3, 1987. My thanks, also, to Myrtle Tostoworyk, now retired Executive Housekeeper, who guided me on a tour of the whole hotel.

Finally, I acknowledge the co-operation of Tim Lilburn, writer in residence, consultant, at University of Western Ontario, 1989 and all others whose support and encouragement helped me along the way.

PUBLISHER'S MESSAGE

This publication marks the first major attempt to document in print some of the remarkable history of one of Canada's, and indeed, the world's most exceptional hotels. Much more than a splendid hostelry, the Château Laurier's French château style of architecture and the hotel's prominent location in the Nation's Capital have long complimented the adjacent Federal Parliament Buildings. Perhaps that is as it should be, as countless important political decisions have been made within the hotel, resulting in the Château's other name "The Third Parliament"!

Meet Me At The Château consists of many stories of the past and numerous vintage photographs. In compiling material for this book, author, Joan Rankin has been assisted by a number of individuals and organizations, to whom she has already expressed appreciation. As her publisher, I wish to add my thanks to all. An earnest attempt has been made to check and verify the information contained in this book. Any errors or omissions brought to the author's attention will be corrected in subsequent editions.

The cooperation of Mr. Peter Howard and his staff, especially Sandi Digras, has made a formidable publishing project both easier and additionally enjoyable. I wish to acknowledge also, the interest and cooperation of Karsh of Ottawa, in particular Yousuf and Estrellita Karsh, to whom their Château home and family mean so much.

To art director/designer Steve Eby and Natural Heritage's editor-in-chief, Jane Gibson, I extend my thanks and add compliments on their invaluable contribution.

A further word of appreciation is due to Dr. Paul Bator, Historical Consultant to the Ontario Heritage Foundation, for his encouragement and helpful editorial recommendations.

Meet Me At The Château continues this publisher's commitment to the quality production of Canadiana in print.

THE EARLY YEARS

*At the turn of the century a
spectacular hotel is built through
the foresight and faith of a
controversial man
of action.*

DREAMS, SKULDUGGERY
AND TRAGEDY

How did a spectacular French Gothic style hotel come to be built in turn-of-the-century Ottawa? Who had the foresight and faith in the future of this country to plan for the time when Ottawa, as Canada's Capital, would become the focal point of our national, political and social life?

Charles Melville Hays, an American, was a controversial man, a man of action. To many, he was an unscrupulous rogue. Bearded, with intelligent but shrewd eyes, he first came to Canada in 1896 as the General Manager of the Grand Trunk Railway of Canada. The Company Chairman, Sir Charles Rivers-Wilson, had been impressed by the work of William Van Horne of the Canadian Pacific Railway. If that was the aggressive type Canadians wanted to run their railways, he would find such an individual for the Grand Trunk. His friend, J. Pierpont Morgan, a leading American banker and railroad director, recommended Hays. At age thirty-seven, Hays had already made a name for himself in the United States by advancing rapidly in the employ of several American railroads. Most recently his revamping of the Wabash Railway had turned it into a most successful operation. Hays accepted the Grand Trunk's offer and arrived in Montreal with his wife, Clara, and their four daughters.

The Grand Trunk had dual business offices. The Chairman, Board of Directors and shareholders were all wealthy Englishmen who dictated policy from head offices in London, England. The actual running of the railroad, however, was the task of the General Manager and staff at the Canadian head office in Montreal. Once a year Rivers-Wilson came to Canada on an inspection tour. He would board his private business car and cover the route, usually accompanied by Hays or one of his assistants.

After Hays had been in Montreal for some time, a *Montreal Standard* reporter described him in these words:

"He gets to his office at seven a.m. and quits at night when the dynamo gives out. He is a fine fat little man, is Charles Hays, and energetic? Say! Ordinary energy acts like placid inertia compared with his brand of hustle!"[1]

Charles Melville Hays.

Hays and Rivers-Wilson were complete opposites. The Chairman, always a gentleman, approached matters in an indirect way and only took action after giving considerable thought to a problem. Hays prided himself on jumping right into a situation, overriding any resistance from opposition. Often he was rude with customers, all of whom were looking for preferential treatment of their goods carried over G.T.R. lines. In negotiations with the Laurier government he lacked the skill of give and take. As well, Hays sometimes completely misrepresented his company's position in order to further his own ambitions.

In 1900, one tactic Hays used to trick Thomas Shaughnessy, President of the Canadian Pacific Railway, deeply shocked the London Board. Survey crews and right-of-way buyers were sent into northern Wisconsin. It was to appear as though the crews were doing preliminary work to extend Grand Trunk lines from Chicago into Manitoba. When Hays was satisfied that the rival line had taken notice of these proceedings, he approached them and offered to exchange running rights over all Grand Trunk lines in Eastern Canada in exchange for the same privileges across more than one thousand miles of C.P.R. tracks covering the wilderness north of Lake Superior. Shaughnessy, however, was too wary to be caught by that ruse. The offer was turned down. Hays left the company in a huff over the matter. Eighteen months later he returned. Rivers-Wilson must have believed he would come back, as he did not replace him in his absence.

Not surprisingly, Hays cared little for the welfare of company employees and, in 1910, he refused to offer them parity with U.S. railwaymen. His action precipitated a bitter strike during which Hays fired the strike leaders. When a settlement was finally reached, he failed to keep his promise to reinstate the fired workers. Frequently, he let his Chairman down, yet for some curious reason, Rivers-Wilson remained loyal to his manager. Repeatedly Hays was told to stick to running the railroad as it was and leave policy to the British Board. With their expectation of 'Not Growth but Dividends', there was no intention of expansion.

In spite of warnings from London, Hays was determined to expand the line. He kept buying smaller lines to link with Grand Trunk Railroad (G.T.R.), obtaining more track moving westward, trying to forge a second transcontinental rail system. In the process he did everything he could, no holds barred, to edge out the western entrepreneurial team of William Mackenzie and Donald Mann, who were also pushing west with their railway, the Canadian Northern. Sir Wilfrid Laurier tried repeatedly to get the two firms to join forces to form one good line, but Hays dismissed the westerners as two adventurers not to be trusted.

As well as Hay's desire to see the railway reach the west coast, he also dreamed of several excellent railway stations and deluxe hotels to be built in major cities across Canada, to serve the needs of the travelling public.

At this time, numerous independent railways ran in and out of Ottawa. The first central rail depot had been built by J.R. Booth in 1895. Booth's style was to play tough by placing obstacles in the way of other railways and attempting to bar them from access to the station via the Interprovincial Bridge. On January 1, 1905, Booth sold Canada Atlantic to Grand Trunk, but the original name was used until 1914. Despite the sale, Booth continued to behave as though the depot existed for his own personal use. Such behaviour upset both his competitors who believed it to be a public facility and the City Council who had paid Booth $50,000 to complete the station on time.

Charles Hays wanted to end all that. He envisioned a large central railway station, architecturaly pleasing, and nearby, the finest hotel yet to be built in Canada. The hotel was to be eminently suitable for the Capital city of the Dominion of Canada. Land was already available for the station. That section of property between Laurier Bridge on Laurier Avenue, then Theodore Street, and Sapper's bridge on Rideau Street had been included in the Grand Trunk purchase of Booth's depot.

On April 27, 1907, the Grand Trunk incorporated the new Ottawa Terminals Railway Company for the purpose of constructing the railway station and hotel for Ottawa. With Charles Hays as President of this company, the funding was to be provided by the Grand Trunk.

Hays had his eye on the southwest corner of Major's Hill Park, the portion that faced Rideau Street, as a suitable site for the hotel. This beautiful park, named for Major Daniel Bolton, resident engineer officer for the Rideau Canal after 1832, ran north from Wellington Street to the Ottawa River in a long, narrow corridor of land bounded by the Rideau Canal on the west side and Mackenzie Avenue on the east. The hotel would stand directly across the street from the railway station and the two buildings would be linked by an underground tunnel. Sir Wilfred Lauirer took a keen interest in the project. Such prestigious buildings could only add stature and dignity to the capital!

With government support assured, Hays approached the Ottawa City Council for their co-operation. He told the Council, "I have never been to Ottawa without thinking that the approach to the city should be an impressive one; one which would welcome people to our nation's Capital."[2] He offered to build a new station, to be known as the Central Union Passenger Station, at a cost of $250,000. The hotel, to be called the Château Laurier in honour of Sir Wilfrid Laurier, would cost between $1,250,000 and $1,500,000. In return he asked the city to grant a fixed assessment of $150,000 on the station and one not to exceed $200,000 on the hotel for a period of twenty years.[3]

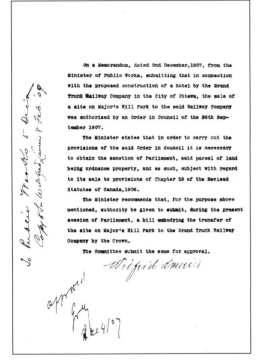

At the government level, an Order-in-Council on September 26, 1907 authorized the sale of the site on Major's Hill Park. Because it was Government Ordinance property, the transfer of the land to the Grand Trunk Railway Company had to be submitted for Crown approval. The cost of land to the G.T.R. was to be $100,000.

Strict conservation measures were imposed by the Government. The Department of Public Works defined the boundaries of the ground to be used for the hotel with prominent stakes. The company or contractors would then erect a fence on the boundary line, which the Department must approve. No building materials could be piled outside the fence, and the stone for use in the building must be cut and prepared away from Major's Hill Park. Carting materials and driving them over any of the park pathways outside the fence was strictly forbidden. None of the trees in the park was to be used to hold guy lines, nor were any trees to be cut down. If any should be in the way inside the fence, they were to be carefully uprooted and replanted in another section of the park. Finally, any damage done by the contractors to the grass plots, trees or walks during construction was to be repaired. All parklands were to be restored to their original condition.

The Minister of Public Works' final recommendation stated, as a condition of sale to the railway, that the hotel must be constructed within two years from the date of the grant and that construction must be according to plans approved by the government. If the construction did not take place within that set period, then the property would revert to the Crown.

The memorandum was signed by the Minister of Public Works, with Sir Wilfrid Laurier signing the Privy Council request to London, England. On July 20, 1907, the agreement was ratified and the Order-in-Council confirmed by His Majesty King Edward VII, on the advice of and with the consent of the Senate and the House of Commons.

Opposition to the sale of Major's Hill property came fast and furious. Some people thought that laying the cornerstone in a month's time was too long; others thought it too soon. Some felt the two year period was too long. Others bemoaned the loss of the parkland.

Sir Wilfrid Laurier had answers for most of the critics. To those who were concerned about losing the beautiful park, he pointed out the fact that not a single tree outside the fence could be destroyed. To those others who feared that the approach to the hotel would convert their lovely Major's Hill Park into a thoroughfare for handling supplies and even garbage, the Prime Minister replied that, according to the specifications, all traffic was forbidden through the park. It must be conducted along the present roadway leading down to the canal docks. The contractors added that the road would, of course, become a subway, as the entire space between the station and hotel was to be turned into a level plaza. With that, some were silenced. This area is now Rideau Street. To the south-west of the hotel is Confederation Square where the National War Memorial now stands.

Still others made a moral issue of the underground tunnel to be built between the hotel and station. In 1953 Madge Macbeth, of the *Ottawa Citizen*, wrote in an article reflecting on this period of Ottawa's history:

> "Such a tunnel, dark and devious, where police would not be in evidence and removed from the general flow of traffic, would attract pick-pockets and, worse still, gentlemen whose misdemeanours were of a far more serious nature. Such a tunnel would be a menace." [4]

Regarding those who feared the tunnel would be a health hazard, her column continued:

> "The tunnel could be cold, hot, damp, or dry. It would be airless. A germ mislaid along its length could not possibly find its way to freedom. It would lurk in some dark corner and leap upon an unsuspecting victim. The tunnel would, indeed, be a menace."

Noted Ottawa Journalist Madge MacBeth photographed by
Yousuf Karsh in 1936.

The most outlandish argument reported was that of the faction who said:

> "It is unthinkable that Major's Hill grounds should be converted into a
> backyard for a hotel! Think of your own backyard magnified ten times or
> more. Think of the garbage pails, the children's sand piles, and worse,
> think of the clotheslines stretching from tree to tree."

A vivid picture was painted of 'long, white, woollen underwear
(male), dancing drunkenly in the wind, or stiffening in 30 degrees below
zero weather, in strange angles that would never fit a human leg'. They
visualized 'black stockings (female), that writhed against billowing
petticoats of every variety and colour, from lace-trimmed nainsook (a
fine, soft cotton fabric) to practical brown sateen'. [5]

All this turmoil over 'washing' could have been avoided if attention had been given to the interpretation of the word 'lines'. Clotheslines never appeared in the conditions of sale. The discussion had been over guy lines, or ropes, which were something entirely different.

The man whom Charles Hays commissioned in 1907 to design the Château Laurier and the Central Union Passenger Station was Bradford Lee Gilbert, a distinguished New York architect. His fame had spread across North America, where he was the first to use steel for the construction of the Tower Building in New York. His designs for the Twelfth Street Terminal in Chicago, terminals in Mexico City, Atlanta, Concord and Halifax, as well as his reconstruction of the Grand Central in New York, had firmly established his credentials.

An excellent organizer, Gilbert had a reputation for strict honesty in all his professional dealings. Described as a big man with white hair, a shaggy white moustache and a charming personality, Gilbert began by constructing models of the project.

Colborne Meredith, the bright young architect engaged to represent Gilbert in Ottawa, cleared out one of his Sparks Street offices. He blocked the windows and painted the walls black. Next a dais was erected on which he stood the two plaster models of the hotel and station which had been built by Gilbert in New York and assembled in Ottawa. Azalea plants edged a long mirror set on the floor to represent the Rideau Canal. Behind the three-to-four-foot models, trees and shrubs represented Major's Hill Park. The whole setting measured about nine feet in length. Mr. Gilbert was loud in his praise for his young colleague's ingenuity and artistic conception.

The plans for the new hotel and station were formally approved by Cabinet and sent on to the Governor General for his approval early in October, 1907. It was now time to commence work on both buildings. Down on Little Sussex Street, near the southwest corner of Besserer Street, about two thousand people gathered on the brisk and sunny afternoon of October 26, 1907, to watch Mayor D'Arcy Scott turn the first sod for the building of the station. An engraved silver plate on the Mayor's spade read:

> "Ground was broken with this spade and the work formally started on the Central Union Passenger Station, the train shed, concourse and the baggage annex, by Mayor D'Arcy Scott, Bradford Lee Gilbert, Architect, J. Quinlan and Company, Contractors." [6]

In his speech on that occasion, Scott made mention of the advent of these two great buildings as the next most important event in the life of the city, after the coming of the railways to Ottawa. He paid tribute to Sir Wilfrid Laurier who had taken such great interest in the project. The Mayor went on to publicly thank Charles Hays on behalf of the city, for without his effort and inspiration the buildings would not have been built. Next he gave recognition to Bradford Lee Gilbert as designer of the magnificent edifices. In conclusion he declared the formal commencement of the works according to the plans prepared by Mr. Gilbert and approved by the Government and the City.

Mr. Charles Murphy, solicitor for Mr. Gilbert who was absent that day, alluded to his client as 'one of America's most eminent architects, the man who designed the first steel skeleton structure'. He reminded his audience that:

> "Eighty years ago the Sappers were digging the Rideau Canal on this spot. It is particularly fitting that on the banks of that great work there should now be begun an enterprise meaning so much to the advancement and beautification of the city." [7]

The hotel's construction site in 1909.

He continued with numerous compliments for Colborne Meredith, who was to supervise the work.

Colborne Meredith, known as 'Colly' to his family and friends, was born to Edmund and Fanny Meredith in St. Andrew's, New Brunswick, in September 1874 while his family was on vacation from Ottawa. He attended the University of Toronto and, in the summer of 1892, apprenticed as a student of architecture to Mr. Frank Darling, the outstanding Canadian architect of his time, a partner in the firm of Darling, Currie, Sproatt and Pierson. Meredith stayed with the firm until he graduated, then moved as a full-fledged architect to Ottawa where he soon acquired recognition for his extensive professional knowledge.

There was no doubt that Charles Hays had chosen the best men to bring to fruition his vision of a splendid French Gothic style château for Ottawa and a classically beautiful Central Union Passenger Station.

But something went wrong. In 1907 the Ottawa Terminals Railway Company had been granted two years in which to erect the two buildings. But

Progress at last.

opening date was not until June 1, 1912! What happened to delay the work by more than two years? *The Architectural Record*, in 1908, tells us:

> "After Mr. Hays had secured the agreement of the Governor-in-Council to the execution of the plans, and that of the City Council of Ottawa on the score of the 'Final and irrevocable decision' of his company to spend $2,500,000 on the improvement of Ottawa to the 'fixed assessment' — after these things were secured, and six days before the plans were to be submitted to the City Council for final adoption, he instructed his architect by telegraph, to cut down the plans so as to save a million dollars. This was done, as it had to be, by such drastic measures as the omission of entire stories from each of the buildings, to their grievous injury, practical and architectural. When the revised plans were submitted to the City Council, February 14, 1908, the change did not escape notice, and an observant Councilman inquired whether these plans would cost $2,500,00 to execute. Mr. Kelly, the Chief Engineer of the road admitted that they would not, but explained the discrepancy by saying that the Architect had 'exceeded his instructions', though it does not appear that he undertook to explain the discrepancy between the million and a half plans and the two million and a half 'final and irrevocable decision'. But the architect, who happened to be present, promptly resented (these statements) and exposed the misstatement regarding himself. The presentation of plans which would cost but a million and half, by a corporation which had announced its 'final and irrevocable' purpose to spend two million and a half was a circumstance which, when one noted, required explanation. It was the pliant architect who was relied upon to furnish this difficult explanation. When he declined to certify that plans out of which he had just cut a million dollars would cost the amount of his original estimate, and when he showed hesitation about galloping into the wilderness as a scapegoat laden with all the incompatibilities of statement of the officers of the Grand Trunk and the Ottawa Terminals, then these august corporations had no further use for so unpliant a designer. Exit, accordingly, at this point, Mr. Bradford Lee Gilbert. Enter, accordingly, only a little later, that egregious Canadian architectural firm of Messrs. Ross and Macfarlane.

Only a little later. For the hearing before the City Council at Ottawa at which Mr. Gilbert had displayed his incompatibility with the requirements of the projectors, his employers, was on February 14, 1908. And it was on May 15th that the elastic and undiscouraged Vice-President Hays re-bobbed up serenely before the City Council of Ottawa with a 'new' set of plans, estimated to cost 'for the hotel and appurtenances something in excess of $1,500,000,' and for the station, 'about $525,000.' 'The plans,' he gracefully adds, 'are presented by our architects, Messrs. Ross and Macfarlane, of Montreal.'

Remarkable 'new' plans they are. What is most remarkable about them is that, in the intervals between February 14th and May 15th the lightning-like intuition of these British architects had not only traversed the entire field over which the slower-witted American Architect had been painfully plodding for the better part of two years, but in the briefer space they had reached identically the same conclusion as his! As to the hotel, indeed, the cheerful Hays set forth, 'it is substantially in accordance with the plans and models which have been heretofore presented and which I understand were satisfactory'. Not quite identical, for our 'new' architects have had the happy thought, for example, of turning all the bathrooms inward upon a dark corridor instead of giving them outside light and air. Not quite identical exteriorly, for they have here had the happy thought of cheapening the execution at the trifling sacrifice of the artistic character of the detail. As to the station plans, which, the Vice-President sets forth 'are more appropriate in their design and appearance than those heretofore produced,' the appropriateness is far less clear than the appropriation. For in effect, the 'new' station is an amalgam of Mr. Gilbert's ground plan and arrangement with the 'classic' mask which he had originally intended for the station on another site, but had found himself forced to discard when the station was to become a member of an architectural group already committed to Gothic.

There is no use in quibbling about details. We have said that no architect could fail to see that the general lay-out, on so irregular a terrain, and with the necessity of conciliating the new buildings with previous erections, was the gist of the design. No layman, with the photograph of the Government Buildings before him, can fail to see that the block-plan is in fact the design, that the block-plans are identical, that the author of the earlier plan is unquestionably the architect of the work." [8]

The Canadian publication, *Construction Magazine*, entered the controversy by first praising Ross and Macfarlane's plans, saying:

"They are such as to deserve the highest commendation, showing as they do, careful thought and intelligent study, and plainly demonstrating that Canadian architects are fully capable of executing designs and plans for the largest undertakings in regard to new buildings." [9]

This was too much for young Meredith. He wrote to the magazine:

"If you would compare your May and June issues, you will see that Messrs. Ross and Macfarlane cannot be given credit for having originated these designs, and to support my statement, I am sending you photographs of the original accepted plans prepared by Mr. Bradford Lee Gilbert and also those presented by Messrs. Ross and Macfarlane. In justice to Mr. Gilbert, I will ask you to publish these photos in your next issue so that the profession may be in a position to judge for themselves whether under the circumstances, Ross and Macfarlane are to be commended for their action." [10]

Construction did publish the designs of both firms in their August 1908 edition. The editor said:

"In the opinion of *Construction* there is no reason why work of this nature should go to foreign architects. We maintain that originally this work should have gone to some Canadian designer. It is, however, not quite clear to us that the religious adherence to the policy of giving preference to Canadian architects should blind us to any infraction of the basic principle of professional ethics."

The magazine agreed that Mr. Gilbert has been conscientious in the performance of his duties and should have been treated with professional decency.

Meredith later stated:

"I was fortunate in being the Canadian representative for Bradford Lee Gilbert of New York, who designed the Château Laurier and the Union Station. I did much of the preliminary work here (in Ottawa), for him and fought a pretty brisk battle for him when the work was stolen by Ross and Macfarlane. The first foundation work on the station was carried out under my direction. The Château was started some months later." [11]

Despite this public controversy over professional ethics, nothing changed.

In February, 1910, work on the Château and Station was resumed under the direction of Ross and Macfarlane. Contracts for construction of the Château were awarded to several firms. The Dominion Bridge Company of Montreal became responsible for furnishing and erecting the structural steel for the two buildings. The Garth Company of Montreal supplied and installed the plumbing, steam fittings, and heating and ventilation systems, as well as manufacturing and installing the brass mail chutes and boxes used in the Château. Additionally, they supplied brine heating and coils for the tunnel. Bishop Construction, also of Montreal, was responsible for the construction of pipe tunnel trenches and sewers running from the hotel to the station. On September 16, 1909, the George A. Fuller Company Limited of New York City, was contracted for:

"...the erection and completion ready for delivery to the Company (Ottawa Terminals Railway Company), of the building known as the Château Laurier at Ottawa, with the exception of the steel material required therefor."

A second contract went to the Fuller Company in July, 1911, for the erection of a terrace on the west side of the Château, over the tracks of the C.P.R. and the Hull Electric Railway. In September, 1911, the Major's Hill Taxicab and Transfer Company reached an agreement with the G.T.R.:

"...for the carrying and operating of a taxicab and vehicular transfer service in the City of Ottawa, in connection with the G.T.R.'s Château Laurier Hotel, now under construction, and will provide taxicab service and transfer service in connection with said hotel."

The beautiful marble work for the stairs and lavatories was under contract to Smith Marble and Construction Company Limited in Montreal. Peter Lyall and Sons were the general contractors for the station, and James Ballantyne installed the plumbing and steamfitting in the new Baggage Annex Building.[12]

While all this was going on in Canada, Sir Charles Rivers-Wilson retired from the Grand Trunk in 1909. Charles Hays succeeded him as President. Financing difficulties with the Grand Trunk Pacific (the western section of the Grand Trunk) took him to London several times to account for his actions to the Board. While there, he studied the architecture of England's great hotels, and went on to the continent to learn about hotel management in western Europe, in preparation for the building of other deluxe hotels in Canada.

On one such trip in April, 1912, Hays was accompanied by his wife, Clara, their daughter, Margaret, a second daughter and son-in-law, Mr. and Mrs. Thornton Davidson, Mrs. Hays' maid, Miss Anne Perrault, and Hays' private secretary, Mr. Vivian Payne. All were invited by Hays' friend, J. Bruce Ismay, Chairman of the White Star Steamship Lines, to return with him to New York aboard his brand new steamship on its maiden voyage from Southampton on April 10, 1912. The ship was the Titanic.

Hays' family and fellow first-class passengers enjoyed luxurious accommodations and the best meals master chefs could produce. Like Hays, many of the men carried on business as usual. Ship radios kept them in touch with their offices in New York and London. During one after-dinner conversation on the evening of April 14, Hays is reputed to have suggested that the intense competition among shipping companies to build faster and larger ships would someday soon lead to a disaster at sea. Scant hours later, his prophecy came true.[13]

In his haste to reach New York in record time, Titanic Captain Edward J. Smith had ignored numerous and repeated warnings, from other ships in the area, about ice floes and icebergs in the shipping lanes. The hellish ordeal which followed is well known. Although the ship listed severely, many passengers were loath to leave it, still clinging to the notion that it was unsinkable. Crew members were unrehearsed in life-saving drills. They had not been assigned to lifeboats, nor were there enough boats to accommodate all the passengers and crew. Charles Hays and others tried to assist passengers to the ship's side and, from there, to the few boats in the sea below. Mrs. Hays, her daughters and her maid were among the five hundred people fortunate enough to reach safety, plucked from the frigid waters of the North Atlantic by other ships in the vicinity. Charles Hays, his son-in-law, his secretary and fifteen hundred others perished. Hays' prediction could not have been more accurate.

An early view of the hostelry that upon completion was to be hailed as the finest hotel yet built in Canada.

Chapter Two

THE DREAM COMPLETED

SHOCK WAVES REVERBERATED across Europe and North America over the loss of the Titanic. Whole nations were in mourning. Social events on both sides of the Atlantic were postponed for months. Celebrations planned in Ottawa for the opening of the Château Laurier Hotel and the Central Union Passenger Station were cancelled out of respect for Charles Hays.

Although a controversial business figure, Hays had many friends. Memorial services were held for him in London, England and in Montreal. During the time of the Montreal service, held at the American Presbyterian Church Hays had attended since his arrival there, the entire Grand Trunk system, and railway and steamship lines throughout Canada, Britain and the United States, came to a complete halt for five minutes of silent tribute. The following week Hays' body was recovered from the sea and finally laid to rest.

The tragedy of the Titanic had not yet occurred when Frederick W. Bergman, Hays' General Manager of Grand Trunk Hotels and the first manager of the Château Laurier Hotel, arrived in Ottawa. German born, Bergman brought with him invaluable hotel management experience gained in the U.S.A.

In 1911 he opened an office in the still-unfinished Château. His American wife and their two small daughters also moved into the hotel. They had a harrowing time coping with the hazards of open elevator platforms and other construction dangers until the building of the hotel was complete. Four employees made up the original office staff. Among them was a secretary named Marjorie Fair, later Mrs. Marjorie Garden. Much later, as a senior resident of St. Patrick's Home, she recalled:

"The office staff consisted of Mr. Bergman, the Manager, Mr. Finch, Chief Engineer, Mr. Howorth, Chief Steward and myself, as secretary. In April of 1912 we were all awaiting the arrival of Mr. Charles Hays from England. He was coming to Ottawa to preside over the opening ceremonies at the Château Laurier and the Central Union Passenger Station. Suddenly we received the ghastly news of the sinking of the Titanic, made even more horrible for us because of the loss of Mr. Hays. We were all terribly shocked. All thoughts of celebrations went out of our heads and Mr. Bergman postponed the openings until June." [1]

The Grand Trunk had commissioned the French sculptor, Paul Chevre, to create a marble bust of Sir Wilfrid Laurier for display in the lobby of the hotel bearing his name. Plans for a public unveiling of the completed work were replaced with a private viewing for this honoured statesman on the day before the hotel was to open. It was anticipated that Laurier would have been as delighted with the bust as he had been with everything else he had seen in the Château. Instead, he was outraged. The nose, he protested, in no way resembled his own. Mr. Bergman confessed that the sculpture had been dropped by one of the workmen carrying it into the hotel, and the nose was chipped. A local sculptor immediately repaired it, but his work was apparently unsatisfactory for Laurier left the hotel an angry man. Despite all the furor, the first person to sign the guest register was Sir Wilfrid Laurier.

At seven o'clock in the morning of June 1, 1912, the doors of both the hotel and station were finally opened without ceremony. A steady stream of

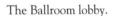

The Ballroom lobby.

View of the drawing room.

Ottawa's leading businessmen and interested residents toured the buildings throughout the day. They had watched the metamorphosis of steel and stone from stark slabs into the dream castle on the north side of the street and into a classically elegant structure, the Station, on the south side. The vision was realized.

Union Station, as it came to be known, was an impressive structure of utilitarian design reflecting its function. Constructed of Indiana limestone, it was a square, dome-topped building embraced by classical stone pillars. A large bronze canopy hung over the main entrance, shielding it from inclement weather. Inside, a broad corridor led to a marble staircase. At the foot of the stairs, the general waiting room, rising four storeys to a high vaulted ceiling, was comparable in size to that found in Grand Central Station in New York City.

The Governor General retained his own suite in the station, where he greeted Royals and other notable visitors to the city. As well, a large display area, available for use by commercial travellers, was a first for any Canadian railway station.

The Château Laurier Hotel typified the grandeur of the old châteaux seen in the Loire Valley in France. It was built of smooth granite blocks and light-buff Indiana limestone. Its crown, erupting with turrets, dormers and gables, was sheathed in copper which the elements would slowly oxidize to a soft shade of green to match the roofs of the Parliament Buildings next door.

Living room, Wren suite.

Hotel lobby with marble bust of Sir Wilfrid Laurier.

Inside, the lobby with its richly panelled and molded ceilings recalled the period of Francis I of France. The floors of Caen stone were trimmed with Napoleon-grey and Belgian-black marble. Authentic Tiffany windows, a finely etched stone fireplace and a marble drinking fountain added their elegance. The Palm or Tea Room opened onto the lobby. Here the Caen-stone walls and tile floors were enhanced with antique-green trim. Private afternoon tea parties hosted by Ottawa's society ladies were frequent events. Nearby, simple Flemish-style oak wainscoting and plaster ceiling friezes and cornices decorated a gentlemen's lounge.

The Main Dining Room, which faced Major's Hill Park, was distinguished from the other public rooms by its Elizabethan restraint. A large mural depicting the period hung over the fireplace. Hotel offices were on the main floor. The ladies' lounge, rented offices, salons and board rooms were accommodated on the mezzanine.

The original dining room was situated at the end of Peacock Alley.

A marvellous view of the park and the Ottawa River, from windows extending the full height of the room, was the main feature of the banquet room. From there one proceeded into the ballroom foyer and the ballroom itself, a magnificent space seventy feet long and forty feet wide. All three of these areas were furnished in the mode of Louis XVI. Five other separate dining rooms made it possible for hotel staff to serve six banquets simultaneously. A State apartment and other special rooms, which could be converted into suites as the need arose, completed the first floor.

The next four floors each consisted of fifty-eight bedrooms. Since only one hundred and fifty-five of the three hundred and two bedrooms had private bathrooms, common bathrooms had been built beside rooms ending in numbers twenty-five and forty-four on each floor.

It was typical of hotels in the early 1900's to provide dormitory accommodation for those who could not afford private rooms. The Château was no exception. There were two dormitories for men and five for women on the sixth floor, with a bathroom convenient to each. Travelling salesmen often occupied the remaining thirty-seven rooms on this level and other rooms on the next floor. Sample rooms were available for the salesmen to display their company products.

Assistant Housekeepers had permanent residences on the seventh floor, as did the Executive Housekeeper who was provided with her own suite. Live-in housemaids were housed two-to-a-room on the eighth floor. The remaining space on this level was used for storage.

The local firm of Cleghorn and Beatty won the carpet and drapery contract for the Château and the Governor General's suite in the station. So proportioned were the corridors and stairs in the hotel that broadloom for these areas had to be made on special looms in Glasgow, Scotland. The strips, six feet wide and three hundred feet long, were each woven in one continuous, seamless piece and finished with a border on both sides. Ten thousand yards of material were used to cover two thousand chairs and sofas, each cover chosen to complement the decor of individual rooms and suites.

The basement was a scene of intense activity. It housed the Grill Room, bar, barber shop, shoeshine parlour, and hair-dressing and manicure salons. In another area, the hotel steward supervised the receiving, storing and distribution of hotel supplies. Kitchens also occupied a large portion of the basement, where chefs worked with the most modern equipment of the time in their spotless, white-tiled environments.

Deep in the bowels of the sub-basement, a mini-town existed. Laundry, engineering and electrical departments, staff lounge and dining rooms, locker rooms and repair shops, all shared this space. Skilled craftsmen who could produce a table or chair, or restore damaged furniture to new life worked here.

Bergman soon co-ordinated a staff of no fewer than three hundred and twenty-five men and women. Staff members were rigorously trained, and every employee in contact with the public was inspected at the beginning of each shift for personal grooming and fresh uniforms. More than one occasion of carelessness was cause for dismissal. The manager brought with him experienced staff from the United States who, in turn, trained local people.

In time the Château workforce became a family affair. Men and women employed in the hotel in the earliest days were joined by their sons and daughters when they came of working age. Emile Labranche, a forty-year veteran of the Château, recalled:

> "My father was one of the first employees of the Château Laurier. He worked in the engineering department, and knew all the inside workings of the hotel. There were seven boys in our family, and as each one became old enough to work, my father got him a job at the Château. We even had a sister and an aunt and uncle who worked there." [2]

On the evening of the hotel opening, Mr. Bergman entertained members of the Canadian and American press, who viewed the accomplishments as outstanding. That same evening, numerous Ottawa citizens revelled in the luxury of the new main dining room. Ottawans were thrilled with their new hotel and station, which greatly enhanced the appearance of the centre of this, their own Capital city. It became common to hear the phrase, 'Meet me at the Château', whenever teas, dances luncheons or dinners were planned.

The Château was not without competition however. Many people remained loyal to the Old Russell House Hotel, the Windsor and the Grand Union hotels. But it was the Château that would earn an international reputation.

On June 6, 1912, the Canadian Press Association held the first convention hosted by the Château; thousands would follow. Some were booked before the hotel opened. Right on the heels of the Press Association came the Canadian Electrical convention. On June 25, one thousand members of the American Library Association converged on Ottawa. The Ballroom, banquet rooms and private dining rooms were all in full swing.

Social events began to flourish in the new setting. The hotel soon became a favourite 'coming out' place for local debutantes who enjoyed lavish receptions in the ballroom in the presence of the Governor General and his wife. Young ladies dressed in fashionable white gowns, elaborately trimmed with trains, long white kid gloves and head-dresses of white ostrich plumes, spent an evening dining and dancing with the sons of Ottawa society. Mrs. Lord, granddaughter of pioneer landowner and timber baron, Philoman Wright, brought out her own granddaughter, Lois Scott, at the Château.

Gradually, the elegant service appointments and superior cuisine attracted a loyal clientele. Members of Parliament, Senators and Ambassadors made the hotel their home away from home at rates reduced from the regular $3.50 per diem charge for a deluxe room.

Even Sir Wilfrid Laurier frequented the hotel, having forgotten his anger about the marble bust. As the story goes, one day while he waited in the lobby for a friend, he was noticed by a young American woman. She looked with interest from Laurier to the bust beside him for several minutes before remarking on the likeness. Laurier removed his hat and bowed deeply. The young lady gasped, "Why, it's almost the image of you!" "Madame," said he, "I fear it is very much like me."

Just weeks after the opening of the hotel and station, construction was undertaken to form the plaza between them, to be known as Connaught Place. In this operation, the Dufferin and Sappers' Bridges had to be demolished. Dismantling the former proved simple enough, but the old Sappers' Bridge refused to budge, attesting to the durability of Colonel By's great work.

The *Ottawa Free Press* had this to say about the operation:

> "So hard was the stone and so clinging and steel-like the grip of the ancient cement, that even dynamite failed to wreck it. As a last resort, the contractors used a derrick to hoist up a block of stone weighing about two tons, to a height of fifty feet and then dropped it on the bridge. For three and a half hours it withstood the terrible battering. Finally, one last blow carried the entire bridge into the canal. The noise resounded over the city like the boom of a great gun." [3]

The Great War

Two years after the Château Laurier opened, Britain declared war against Germany. In 1914 Canada quickly rallied to the aid of her mother country. Colonel Sam Hughes, Prime Minister Borden's Minister of Militia and Defence in Ottawa, called for volunteers from across the country to serve in Canada's army overseas. He was determined to form a Canadian contingent with a Canadian command, to fight alongside the British in France. The response was overwhelming.

A flamboyant and erratic character, Sam Hughes lived at the Château during the war. He worked swiftly and took credit for most decisions made by his department. Always the first man in the hotel dining room when it opened at six a.m., he never left the building for his office later than six thirty. His staff car and driver were a familiar sight in front of the hotel. Although Hughes would not return until well after midnight he, nevertheless, left a wake-up call for five o'clock each morning.

Col. Sam Hughes.

Waiting for the Minister of Militia and Defence.

On July 15, 1916, Sir Robert Borden, as Prime Minister of Canada, was given a welcome home reception at the Château on his return from England. He had attended a meeting of the British Cabinet, a precedent-setting gesture of the British Government. Never before had anyone other than a British Minister taken part in a Cabinet meeting on the same footing as one of its members. He had also visited Windsor Castle, where he had a long conversation with His Majesty King George V about the war. Such happenings made great grist for the war-time media.

During World War I the Canadian railways were urgently needed for the transportation of men and supplies. But all the large, privately operated railways, with the exception of the Canadian Pacific Railway, were so deeply in debt as a result of overextension it was thought they might have to cease operations. As an emergency measure, the government stepped in and took over operation of the troubled lines. In 1919, after the war was over, Parliament passed an Act creating a new railway company owned by the people of Canada. This company was called the Canadian National Railways. Along with the railways it now controlled, Canadian National Railways (C.N.R.) inherited several hotels from its predecessors, including the Château Laurier. These hotels formed the C.N.R. hotel chain, a division of the C.N.R.

Despite the war and lack of clientele from overseas, the Château was very popular with Americans from bordering states. The opportunity to indulge in the opulent atmosphere of a world-class hotel so close to home was frequently enjoyed. For the people of Ottawa, the Château was the site of fund-raising events in aid of the war effort. Despite the times social occasions were frequent. The scrap books of poet and socialite Duncan Campbell Scott and his wife, Belle Botsford Scott, contain numerous invitations such as these:

Counsul General of Japan
At Home
Wednesday, November 10, 1915
in honour of the
Coronation of His Majesty
the Emperor of Japan

Mme. Landry
At Home
4 April 1916
Château Laurier

Royal Society of Canada
and
Conference of Canadian Universities
will dine at the Château Laurier
23 May 1917 [4]

Work was available for young people at the Château during World War I while many of the regular employees fought overseas. Mrs. Barbara Williams in Carp, Ontario, tells us this story about her father, Jack Ballard:

"Dad was a young lad who emigrated to Canada from England in 1909 with his mother and family after the death of his father. They had very little money and Dad had to work. He was working for a prominent Ottawa electrical firm until one evening he was told to go to an address in the west end of the city, far from his home, to do some repair work. He agreed to do so if he could borrow five cents for streetcar fare. His tools were too heavy to walk the distance. No one at the shop gave him the nickel, so he went home without carrying out the request. Next morning, he was fired for not doing as he was told.

After several unsuccessful attempts to find work, Dad discovered his former employer had passed the word along to other electrical firms that young Ballard could not be depended upon and should not be hired. Desperate for work, Dad timidly approached Mr. Tom McGrail, who was hiring at the Château Laurier. He explained his predicament, and Mr. McGrail said he would take him on probation for two weeks. If in that time he did what he was told, he could stay; if not he would be fired. My father's work must have been very satisfactory, as he retired from the Château Laurier fifty-five years later. He worked his way up to be Chief Electrical Engineer and knew every wire in the hotel. Because of poor health in his later years, Dad gave up the responsibility of the Chief Engineer's position, and reverted to a staff electrician until his retirement in 1969."[5]

Jack Ballard, the Château's chief electrical engineer, worked in the hotel for 55 years.

A disastrous fire destroyed the Centre Block of the Parliament Buildings in Ottawa on the night of February 3, 1916. Seven people lost their lives. Because it was wartime, sabotage was suspected but never proved. Electrical specialists were convinced the blaze was likely caused by old, faulty wiring. Only the Library of Parliament was spared when library clerk, Connolly MacCormac, had the presence of mind to bolt the steel fire door separating the library from the Centre Block.

Grattan O'Leary, then an editorial writer with the *Journal* and later its publisher, reminisced about his experience that night as follows:

"One of the bizarre episodes of the First World War was the Parliament Buildings' fire in February, 1916. I was at a dinner given by the Minister of Militia, Sir Sam Hughes, at the Château Laurier. His dinners were not dry dinners. There were about eight or ten of us there, and one guest from the North of Ireland had a delightful baritone voice. He was in the middle of singing 'Where the Mountains of Mourne Come Down to the Sea' when the door burst open and someone said, 'Good God! What are you people doing here? Don't you know the Parliament Buildings are on fire?' We said, 'We'll go up and put the fire out shortly. Now go away and don't bother us.' But half an hour later someone else came, and we thought we had better have a look. We streamed out to find a pall of black smoke obscuring Parliament Hill and the main tower of the Centre Block shooting great gouts of flame high in the night.

I dashed into the building to get my typewriter and made my way outside through corridors filled with smoke. By this time a great crowd had gathered. It was a bitterly cold night, and people caught in the building were coming down ladders or leaping into the snow beneath the windows." [6]

O'Leary continued:

"When Sam Hughes saw the state of affairs, he summoned the 77th Battalion to aid the City of Ottawa fire-fighters and the government police. The Corps of Engineers, under Colonel Street, cordoned off the buildings to keep back the huge crowd. The fire had begun at nine o'clock. By eleven o'clock, when the Governor General, the Duke of Connaught, arrived with his party from a performance at the Russell Theatre, the fire was at its height, flinging a rippling curtain of flame hundreds of feet over the river.

At three in the morning Sir Sam Hughes reported the fire finally under control. The government held a midnight Cabinet meeting in the

Château Laurier suite of the Minister of Justice, C.J. Doherty. It was decided there would be no interruption in parliamentary sittings. After casting about for other quarters, the government settled on the Victoria Museum, a gaunt Gothic structure built on a swamp on Argyle Avenue in Ottawa."

The End of the Decade

Peace came at last to Canada and the world on November 11, 1918. It was a day for great rejoicing in Ottawa. Connaught Place was jammed with people exhibiting unrestrained joy. A one-thousand-car motorcade assembled at the Plaza, each car decorated with the Union Jack and flags of other allied countries. Bunting festooned both the Château Laurier and Union Station. Throughout the hotel and across the city the celebrating went on well into the night.

This joyful bunting contrasted sharply with the sombre draping that marked the death of Sir Wilfrid Laurier in 1919, bringing sadness to Ottawa and the country at large. On February 22, his lengthy funeral procession moved solemnly from the Parliament Buildings to Notre Dame Basilica. It passed the black-draped Château Laurier and Union Station, where flags flew at half-mast. Thousands lined the snowy streets, their mourning attire a tribute to their sense of loss. This eminent Canadian would be seen no more in the elegant rooms of the Château Laurier, but his warm-hearted spirit, his illustrious name and his marble bust remain to remind us of one of our most loved statesmen.

(Opposite page) Canadian troops march past the Château as they return home following the end of World War I. (Below) A nation mourns as the funeral procession of Sir Wilfrid Laurier passes the Château Laurier Hotel, Feb. 22, 1919.

THE INCOMPARABLE TWENTIES

THE STAGE WAS SET for the unique decade of the 1920's by the cross-Canada tour of His Royal Highness, the Prince of Wales, in the summer of 1919. Arriving in Ottawa on the morning of August 28, he was greeted by the wildest enthusiasm ever witnessed to date in the Capital. Elaborate electrical illuminations adorned the Château for his visit. Included were a blazing torch on one of the hotel towers that was visible for miles and, high up on the front of the hotel, the letters H.R.H. set in green lights. The Prince's crest of silvery-white feathers, outlined with red, blue and green lights, added to the display.

On the evening of November 16, the May Court Club of Ottawa hosted a gala evening with the Prince of Wales as guest of honour. The Governor General and his wife, the Duke and Duchess of Devonshire, and staff members of the vice-regal household were among the guests. Greeting them was Miss Sarah Sparks, May Court President, and a member of a prominent pioneer family in Ottawa. Today Sparks Street, one of Ottawa's main thoroughfares now transformed into a pedestrian boulevard, is a reminder of the prominence of the Sparks' name in Ottawa society.

The May Court Club had been founded in Ottawa in 1898, by Lady Aberdeen, wife of the Governor General, the Earl of Aberdeen, as a service club for women. Eleven clubs were formed in Ontario, each with its own agenda for community work. Some raised funds for women and children's services, such as good nutrition in the schools, while some did volunteer work with children. Today the club in Ottawa operates a convalescent hospital for women.

The first Winter Carnival involving the Château Laurier took place in 1922. The most popular attraction was a wooden slide built between the Château and the Rideau Locks. Made of wood with high sides and filled with ice blocks, it was just wide enough to carry a toboggan. Some dare-devil men skied down this very steep slide on one ski. The toboggans raced down the slope over a series of dips and by the time they reached the river, they were travelling at over one hundred miles an hour. The slogan for the ride was 'Slide a Mile for a Dime'. In an 1984 interview, Gordon Sims, an eighty-three year old Ottawa resident, told reporter Cathy Campbell, "It was quite a slide. A lot of people were afraid of it. It was a fast thing." [1]

The wooden toboggan slide and ice sculpture proved popular with 1922 Winter Carnival participants.

Famous Guests

Men and women of prominence in politics and business in Canada, the U.S.A. and all over the world stayed at the Château Laurier. Mr. Angus Gordon, the Château Laurier manager in 1923, listed some of his famous guests which included: Lord Balfour, Lord Robert Cecil, Lord and Lady Astor, Mrs. Asquith, wife of the former Prime Minister of Great Britain, and General Booth of the Salvation Army. The men and women who worked in the Château gave freely of their time and took great pride in serving the hundreds of guests who were from all walks of life.

Musical Programme [3]

Dinner and Dance, December 12, 1925
Given by Mr. and Mrs. P.D. Ross
To Commemorate the Fortieth Birthday of
The Journal

1. Tenor Solo   In The Garden of Tomorrow   Graffe Dippen

   Mr. Charles Bryson

2. Violin Solo   Am Meer   Schubert-Wilhelmj

   Mr. W.G. Adamson

3. Quartet   (a) Drink To Me Only   Old English

              (b) Going to Press   J.L. Hall

   Messrs:

L.H. Field	1st Tenor
J. Potter	2nd Tenor
R.S. Holmes	1st Bass
F.C. Brown	2nd Bass

4. Bass Solo   Heroes and Gentlemen   Jas. Peskett

   Frank C. Brown

5. Selection by the Château Laurier Orchestra

   At the Piano   Arthur Perry   Song Leader W.M. Gladish

Toasts

The King

The Journal

Mr. Rex Beach, a prominent American novelist of the time, who visited the Château with his wife about twice a year, wrote a glowing letter to Mr. Gordon in which he said he wished it was possible for them to live in New York in a similar hotel.[2]

A dinner and dance typical of many such celebrations held at the Château in the twenties was one given for their staff by the publisher of the *Ottawa Journal* and his wife, Mr. and Mrs. P.D. Ross. The programme for the evening was contained in a folder bearing the Château Laurier crest and the invitation on its cover, while inside were printed the menu and the musical programme.

Love Blossoms at the Château

One member of whom the Château can boast is Danny Lupino who, in 1925 at the age of sixteen, was hired by Mr. Gordon as a bus boy in the Main Dining Room. Danny was the son of Italian immigrants who had settled in Ottawa. Before long, he became a waiter. He talked about his early days at the Château:

> "They put a fancy uniform on me and made me a waiter in the old Main Dining Room. Monsieur Poncet was the headwaiter. My wife, Yvonne, also worked at the hotel before we were married. She was a greenhorn kid, the youngest of sixteen children in a French Canadian farm family from Masham, Quebec. She worked in the kitchen for Chef Amadeo Franci, a real chef, with his hat on the side of his head. He had complete control of the kitchens. Everyone had to behave well, especially the waiters, or the chef would refuse to serve them. If they had no food to carry to the dining room, they had no job.
>
> Chef Franci was good to Yvonne, her sister, and two other girls who worked in the still room where they made salads, cleaned berries, made coffee, and squeezed orange juice. There was no frozen juice then. At breakfast, Yvonne was given a special job in the Main Dining Room. She sat at a table set up in a corner near the entrance to the kitchen which the waiters used. There were two large toasters on the table and a heated cabinet on the floor below the table. As the waiters headed for the kitchen with their orders, they would say, 'Yvonne, I need whole wheat toast, buttered, for two,' or, 'Yvonne, I need two slices of melba toast,' or whatever they needed. Yvonne made the toast, buttered if necessary, put it in a covered dish, then set it in the heated cabinet. She wrapped the dry toast in a napkin after putting it in a rack, then into the cabinet it went. When the waiters returned to pick up their toast, it was always fresh and piping hot."[4]

Danny Lupino added:

"I watched Yvonne make the toast every morning for quite a while. She was dressed in a beautiful white smock and looked as pretty as anything. I thought to myself, 'That's the girl for me.' As a matter of fact, she approached me one day. In the afternoon, we were off duty from two until six p.m., and one day Yvonne said to me, 'Do you ever go to a show?' That's how we began going together."

A New Manager

Mr. Gordon left the Château in 1926. Sir Henry Thornton, President of C.N.R., then hired Joseph Van Wyck as the replacement. Van Wyck had worked in hotels in the U.S., including the old Sherman Hotel in Chicago, before he moved to Vancouver and finally to Ottawa.

Joseph Van Wyck as photographed in 1939 by Yousuf Karsh.

The manager brought two other hotel men with him: John Adam as Maître d'Hotel, and Mr. Helders as Headwaiter in the Grill Room. All three of these men had come originally from Holland. Each of them was viewed as tough, but fair in their dealing with staff.

Danny Lupino recalled:

"Mr. Adam was a real disciplinarian. He walked around wearing a tuxedo, with his bow tie tucked under the corners of his collar. He stood beside the checker's desk where the waiters went by with their trays. If the platters weren't red hot, if the Welsh rarebit wasn't bubbling in the chaffing dish, if you forgot the parsley with the fish or the watercress for the roast beef, he would order you to go back and do it properly.

A little later on, I was offered a job as Captain in another hotel, in Toronto. I thought it would be a good idea to go, but my mother was against it as I was doing well at the Château. I used to go home and empty my tips out of my pockets onto the kitchen table, and give them to my mother. She had very little money and appreciated what I gave her. Yvonne didn't want me to leave Ottawa either, so I consulted with Mr. Adam, who suggested I go and try it, which I did. After a few weeks, I was ready to go back to Ottawa. When I walked into the Château on a Saturday morning and asked Mr. Adam if I could have my job back, he said, 'You start this evening as a waiter in the Grill Room'."

John Helders, the Headwaiter of the Grill Room, as photographed in 1938 by Yousuf Karsh.

Danny concluded:

"Yvonne and I were married in 1928, when we were both nineteen."

One young woman who was interviewed by Mr. Van Wyck for an office position at the Château Laurier, and was successful, was Edith Lancaster. Miss Lancaster talked about that interview:

"I was very impressed by this big Dutchman. He was six foot, two inches tall, had a large head, black hair and dark, piercing eyes. He dressed extremely well. 'Sit down, little girl,' he said, and he proceeded to describe the duties of the position. My job was not only secretarial, but was connected with the catering manager as well. When the latter was off duty from two to five p.m., I had to book functions relating to that department — meeting rooms for organizations and conventions. I had to be especially careful about the dates, as it would be a catastrophe if a meeting, with meals for five hundred or a thousand persons, was booked a day earlier or later. Most of the bookings were made verbally over the counter, or by telephone." [5]

Miss Lancaster's stay developed into a forty-year career. She assisted successive managers until 1962, at which time she became the first Château Laurier Hotel Sales Representative. Although her office was in the Château, she was under

Edith Lancaster, whose secretarial beginnings resulted in a forty-year hotel career, was the Château Laurier's first Sales Representative.

the direction of the Sales Department in Montreal. Her role required travelling by car to the eastern United States, and eastern Quebec and Ontario to secure convention bookings for the hotel. "It was a hard job," she remembered, "but easy in some respects, as I knew the heads of the large corporations and organizations that convened at the Château, and I had no difficulty in making bookings for the hotel." In her first year in this phase of hotel work, she booked over a million dollars worth of business for the Château. Miss Lancaster retired from the hotel in 1967 and continued to live in Ottawa.

The Coming of Radio.

The Château Laurier gained national and international prominence with the advent of radio. As early as May 1920, the Canadian Marconi Company had transmitted an experimental programme to the Château from Montreal, one hundred miles away. A Royal Society audience, including the Right Honourable Sir Robert Borden, Prime Minister of Canada; the Duke of Devonshire, Governor General of Canada; and Mr. Mackenzie King, Leader of the Opposition, listened expectantly to soloists and gramophone records. The reception was recognizable, but not too clear.

In 1923 Sir Henry Thornton became the first Chairman and President of the Canadian National Railways and Hotels. He was an American railroader who had worked for the British rail system during the Great War. Decorated by both the British and the French for his war efforts, Thornton was an excellent choice. Railway workers both liked and admired him.

Sir Henry brought some startling and controversial promotional ideas to the company. Radio entertainment on board trains was one such innovation. This popular move easily transported the post-war nation from the harsh reality of daily life into a fantasy land previously unknown. By June 1923, a Radio Department with offices in the C.N. Express Building on McGill Street in Montreal was established.

The C.N.R. set up numerous telephone connections for microphones and loudspeakers in all the public rooms at the Château so that, later, important addresses could be broadcast directly from the hotel. Every broadcast on station CKCH (the original call letters) had some connection with the hotel.

On that first day of its operations, station CKCH held an open house at its new studios. Many fascinated people took advantage of this opportunity. Others, including this author's father, crowded into the studio after their offices had closed at five. All were eager to learn the mysteries of radio. However, the studio closed to the public at six p.m. to prepare for the evening programme to be broadcast from the Château Laurier.

The lobby of the Château was crowded with visitors eagerly awaiting the commencement of this programme. Ottawans lucky enough to own radios listened in their homes. Members of the Press Gallery received the broadcast in their lounge in the Parliament Buildings. Several Ottawa clubs had loud-speakers installed in their club rooms for the enjoyment of their members. Promptly at eight-thirty p.m., the Château Laurier Orchestra played 'O Canada' to open the programme. This was followed by other 'Patriotic Airs'. Sir Henry declared the station officially open, then addressed the listening audience. He spoke of our wonderful country and invited Americans to come to Canada to see for themselves. He also spoke directly to C.N.R. employees, encouraging them to give their best work and their loyalty to the company. He promised to keep them up to date with developments in the railway world across the breadth of Canada, as well as with the outside world, through the use of radio.

The station was a complete success. Hundreds of local people telephoned congratulations. Telegrams and letters flooded into the station from all over eastern Canada and the eastern U.S.A. after the splendid initial broadcast. Radio had arrived! In July 1924, some five months after its debut, CKCH changed its name to CNRO to indicate it was the C.N.R.'s station in Ottawa.

Château Laurier Dance Orchestra of Canadian National Railways Radio Station CNRO, Ottawa, Canada.

A forerunner of what was to become a great Saturday night institution in Canada, took place in March, 1924 in Ottawa. This hockey broadcast story about a Stanley Cup play-off game was told by Gordon Oliver from the C.N. Radio Department:

"Les Canadiens de Montreal and the old Ottawa Senators were in the finals for the world hockey title. On this occasion, radio station CNRO was linked up by the C.N. Telegraphs to CKAC in Montreal, and I was called upon, on short notice, to forget that I was supposed to be concerned only with technical matters, and to fill in for a sports commentator and to broadcast to the Montreal and Ottawa audiences the proceedings of the Stanley Cup game. It was a battle royal with Les Canadiens winning the game in overtime. At one point, I, a good Montreal supporter, so forget myself as to remark over the air, 'Dirty Ottawa!' Needless to say, a budding career as a sports commentator ended then and there." [6]

CNRO's gala first anniversary birthday party was celebrated on February 26, 1925. Distinguished guests in formal attire gathered in the ballroom of the Château Laurier for a concert, dance, speeches and a six-hour broadcast of festivities, a record for continuous broadcasting.

In the following weeks nearly six thousand congratulatory telegrams and twenty thousand letters were delivered to the station from all over Canada, Newfoundland and many American states. The station staff kept the roses, ate the goodies that poured in, and drew lots for all the other gifts received as congratulations.

One listener from Seal Cove, New Brunswick wrote:

"Congratulations on your first birthday. During the winter your concerts have cheered up so many lonely evenings on this little island in the sea. Radio is a blessing to those who are cut off from city enjoyment. We appreciate the music and the many fine lectures." [7]

Gradually, a nation-wide network of C.N. stations was built up. CNRO was first, then CNRM in Montreal and in 1927 CNRQ, Quebec; CNRT, Toronto and CNRW, Winnipeg.

The Château Laurier was soon to take a more active role in radio broadcasts from Ottawa. When the new wing opened, CNRO moved into the Château from its Bank Street studios. The station occupied the seventh floor in the new wing and is still there today.

The Château Laurier is shown opposite in all its finery, celebrating Canada's Diamond Jubilee in 1927. Among the speakers was Prime Minister William Lyon Mackenzie King.

The Diamond Jubilee

A world record radio broadcast took place in 1927 when Canada celebrated her Diamond Jubilee of Confederation from Dominion Day, Friday, July 1st. through to Sunday, July 3rd. No fewer than twenty-six stations participated in broadcasting the event across the country. Station WWJ in Detroit, Michigan, carried the ceremonies for the benefit of their patrons in the United States. The Marconi beam station, CF, at Drummondville, Quebec, sent the transmission by short wave length to Britain, from there it went by BBC to Europe.

The inaugural concert of the new fifty-three-bell carillon in the Peace Tower on Parliament Hill rang out at eleven forty-five a.m. on July 1st. In the afternoon, ten thousand school children's voices blended in a joyful salute to our country. The Governor General of Canada, His Excellency, Lord Willingdon, addressed the crowd and gave the people a message from His

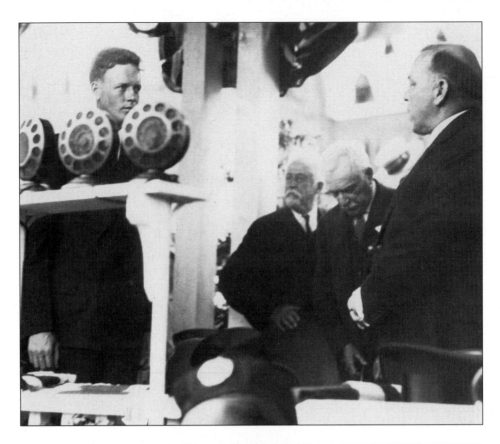

Majesty, King George V. The Prime Minister, Right Honourable Mackenzie King and other politicians also addressed the nation. Lord Willingdon composed a musical score for the Jubilee celebration which was played by the Château Laurier Orchestra during a celebration dinner and concert in the hotel that evening.

Ottawans who attended the festivities on Saturday, July 2nd will never forget the visit that day of Colonel Charles Lindbergh, fresh from his historic non-stop solo flight across the Atlantic from New York to Paris in the *Spirit of St. Louis*. He made a goodwill visit to Ottawa, accompanied by a squadron of twelve United States Air Force planes. All Ottawa seemed to have converged on Uplands landing field on the sandy ground south of the city. People turned it into a family celebration and brought along picnics. Lindbergh, the first to land, was given a thundering welcome. Following this recognition, the Air Force flyers circled in close formation, breaking off one by one to land. Lieutenant J. Thad Johnson, piloting the sixth plane, peeled out of formation and climbed sharply, an act which led to a collision with one of the other aircraft. Johnson bailed out, but his parachute did not have time to open. He was killed when he hit the ground. Instantly, the joy and excitement of the occasion gave way to horror. No one who witnessed that shocking incident, including this author, has ever forgotten that day.

Prime Minister King ordered a state funeral for Lieutenant Johnson to be held the next day. All Jubilee celebrations were cancelled while the city mourned. Because of heavy rain, the service planned for Parliament Hill had to be moved to the auditorium at Lansdowne Park. CNRO staff worked at top speed to move all their equipment in time for the two-thirty p.m. service. They managed it with only two minutes to spare. The radio station picked up the strains of the funeral march being played on the carillon as the body of Lieutenant Johnson was carried to Union Station to be transported to his home in Michigan for burial.

The three-day holiday weekend broadcast, with it joys and sorrows, was estimated to have been heard by five million people. Canadians at home and abroad felt great pride in this exceptional achievement in radio.

Opposite, Prime Minister Mackenzie King welcomes aviator hero Charles Lindberg to Canada's 1927 Diamond Jubilee. Their remarks were enjoyed by some five million Canadians via the 'first' national radio broadcast in Canada. Below, some 40,000 people were in Ottawa to join in the Jubilee celebrations.

In his speech given at the Canadian National Exhibition in Toronto in August of 1927, Prime Minister King commented on that special broadcast:

"On the morning, afternoon and evening of July 1, all Canada became, for the time being, a single assemblage, swayed by a common emotion, within the sound of a single voice. Never before was a national programme enjoyed by the citizens of any land over so vast an area." [8]

A NEW ERA

*By 1929 the enlarged Château
hailed as the 'complete hotel'
was soon to experience
the turbulent years
that followed.*

Chapter Four

THE NEW CHÂTEAU LAURIER

*B*Y THE MID-TWENTIES IT BECAME OBVIOUS that more hotel rooms were needed in Ottawa. Canadian National decided to add a new wing to the Château Laurier, thereby nearly doubling the hotel's capacity to five hundred and fifty rooms and suites from the original three hundred. John S. Archibald of Montreal was chosen as the architect, and John Schofield, the C.N.'s own architect, worked in association with him. Both these men conferred with Mr. Van Wyck who had expertise in successful hotel kitchen planning.

Archibald and Schofield were faced with the challenge of blending the old and the new buildings together so that the charm and beauty of the old would not be lost. The old Château was L-shaped, the long side of which ran parallel to the Rideau Canal to the west, and the shorter front section faced Rideau Street and the Union Station. A turret rose above the angle formed by the two sides. The design not only mirrored the French Château style of architecture, but was an adaptation of the famous Château de Longeais, situated on the Loire River below Tours, France. As Archibald and Schofield designed it, the new east wing was also L-shaped (only an L in reverse) thereby widening the front of the hotel. The long wing ran parallel to the wing on the original building. Thus the two L's became a U shape. The main floor and ground floor filled in the centre of the U, creating a vast improvement to the working core of the hotel.

So skillfully were the old and new melded that the whole structure gave the appearance of having been built at one time, according to one architect's vision. The same limestone was used, rising from the base to eaves, and the same soaring towers repeated. A new central tower, or square keep, with eaves higher than the old roof line, dominated the whole. Joining it to the old was a simple bastion rising to a terrace from which a huge arched opening gave onto the upper storeys of the keep. In the centre of the new wing, on the Mackenzie Avenue side, a circular tower matched one on the original building.

A rather bizarre story has been told about the shiny copper roof on the east wing. It stood out like a neon sign, while the roof on the old building had turned into the lovely soft shade of green that nature's elements bring about on copper through oxidization. The roofing contractor suggested to his workmen that whenever it became necessary for them to urinate while on the job, they do so into a pail. When a pail was full, it was to be dumped over the new copper roof. Mother Nature was thereby given a head start with oxidization. It worked.[1]

A stone canopy protected a direct entrance from Mackenzie Avenue to the Ballroom and Drawing Room. The Governor General and other distinguished guests used this entrance. A second entrance on this side, closer to Rideau Street, gave access to the Grill Room, cafeteria, swimming pool and elevator lobby. The public entered the front of the hotel through a stone portico with arched openings. From there, two solid bronze and glass revolving doors led into the main lobby.

This view of the expanded Château Laurier appeared in the November, 1930 issue of *The Journal*, Royal Architectural Institute of Canada.

Surprise was the first emotion experienced when one entered the new lobby. It looked like an old English baronial hall and was the only room to have strayed from French influence. It has often been said that if you sit in the Château lobby, any day of any week, you are bound to see the great, the notorious, indeed, the whole gamut of human personalities. It has been, over the years, a rich fishing ground for parliamentary correspondents and other media personnel for catching the latest gossip and tips about what was happening on Parliament Hill. Here also friend meets friend and other busy people rush through, oblivious to the atmosphere, only wishing to check in and get to their rooms.

Those who took the time to look around would be impressed by walls of richly carved quarter oak right up to the level of the mezzanine, where a railed gallery afforded an excellent view of the scene below. Art stone completed the wall construction to the ceiling of ornamental plaster, painted in soft greens, rose and deep cream. A floor of Italian travertine marble had hand-cut mosaic inlay in harmonizing colours. Comfortable chairs stood on a red patterned rug. The windows, approximately four feet in height over the front door, were Tiffany's craftsmanship. Tiered candles and wall sconces provided the lighting. Trophies of the hunt, hung from the walls, added to the Old English atmosphere.

Three arched openings led deeper into the hotel and to the reception area, where a long counter of black marble was divided into sections by ornate brass screens for Registration, Inquiries, Mail and Cashier. The elevator corridor and the strikingly beautiful Main Dining Room and Jasper Tea Room corridors were also in the new wing. Prime Minister, the Right Honourable R.B. Bennett conducted his guests to these elevators many times when the Château was his official home.

Roy Rogers and Dale Evans were among the famous Château guests who were quickly whisked to their suites on an elevator reserved for their exclusive use. In 1967, His Majesty, Emperor Haile Selassie was accorded the same privilege when he paid a Centennial year visit to Ottawa. Past the elevators, twin staircases led down to the Grill Room, cafeteria, swimming pool and therapeutic departments.

Double arches to the right off the lobby led into the Convention Hall, the Music Room and a Gentlemen's Lounge. The Music Room was a drawing-room-sized theatre for chamber music. A small stage formed by a graceful arch stood at one end of this salon. The fine acoustics in this room were a great asset

The ornate registration desk in the inner lobby remained unchanged from 1929 to the mid 1980's.

to the numerous artists who wished to visit Ottawa and locate a suitable place for their recitals.

Page Boys and Bellmen

"Calling Mr. C.D. Howe: Calling Mr. F.M. Ross: Calling Miss Elizabeth Smellie," were typical cries heard in the lobbies of the Château Laurier until the end of World War II.

Young page boys, nattily dressed in red and gold tunics with a double row of shiny brass buttons marching down the fronts of their jackets, navy blue pants, red pill-box hats set at a rakish angle on their heads, white-gloved, each carrying a silver tray, searched through the halls, corridors and restaurants for those they were paging. These young lads, who averaged twelve to fourteen years of age, were trained in deportment and taught how to address correctly the people to whom they spoke. These could include a Prime Minister or a famous star, such as Marlene Dietrich. Prior to going on duty each day, pages and bellmen were inspected by the Bell Captain. Each was required to be perfectly groomed.

After World War II, page boys were replaced by bellmen whose main job was to carry luggage to and from the lobby and guests' rooms. Bellmen seemed able to satisfy most requests from patrons, even requests for a bottle of liquor after the stores were closed. They met trains, assisted passengers and greeted dignitaries. Many remained at the Château for over forty years and were good-will ambassadors for the hotel.

More About the Main Floor

The C.N.R. opened what was to become an art gallery and miniature museum of railway transport. This Transportation Room was located in the south-west corner of the main lobby where scenes of Canada decorated the walls. Later, in the thirties, the museum was disbanded and this room became a joint C.N. Railway and Trans-Canada Airlines ticket office with Herman Grierson and Nelson Vermette as the C.N. representatives and Gordon Wood, the first T.C.A. Ottawa Manager.

Adjacent to this room, a spectacular spiral staircase rose in a tower from the floor below to the top floor of the hotel. Walls of Caen stone, marble steps, a polished brass bannister supported by filigreed bronze uprights, and large windows on the tower's outer wall, all attested to the charm of this outstanding example of craftsmanship. Many Ottawa brides have been photographed in all their wedding finery on this exceptional staircase.

A newstand opposite the Transportation Room was always a busy spot and a good place to people-watch for distinguished guests. Grill Room waiter, Danny Lupino, used to pick up boxes of cigars at the stand for guests attending banquets. When a reception was over, he would return any remaining cigars to the clerk on duty and was charged only for the number of cigars used. On Sunday mornings, Ottawans flocked into the lobby to buy the *New York Times* and *Toronto Star*. Many strolled into Peacock Alley to read their papers or simply to watch the world go by.

Peacock Alley, a long, broad corridor, extended along the west side of the hotel, parallel to the Rideau Canal. Enormous leaded glass windows provided natural light in daytime. The walls were panelled in the same type of oak as the lobby and a patterned rug ran the full length of the room. It was comfortably furnished with deep sofas, easy chairs and writing tables. A small lamp on each desk provided good light and atmosphere. Half-way down the Alley, a doorway

Peacock Alley.

led outside to a terrace where a restaurant flourished during the summer months. In the early days, bridal showers and fashion shows were held on this patio.

Afternoon Tea was served from three to six p.m. in Peacock Alley. Charlie Foster, as Captain, and three other waiters looked after this service while James McIntyre's orchestra played in the background. Guests could take advantage of the marvellous view from the Alley. The vista took in the spectacular panorama of the Parliament Buildings, the Rideau Locks and the Ottawa River.

Two new public rooms on the main floor which absolutely delighted guests were the Main Dining Room and the Jasper Tea Room. They faced each other on a main hall. On the right, its entrance guarded by two large Chinese porcelain vases, was the Dining Room. It held approximately two hundred people. Decorated in the Robert and John Adam style, with walls and carpets of apple green, the scene was highlighted by five lofty windows facing east. The morning sun poured in and was reflected at either end of the room by two

The Jasper Tea Room.

ornate mirrors framed in burnished steel. At night three massive chandeliers sparkled from above and additional indirect lighting flooded the room. James McIntyre's group played at lunch and dinner in the Main Dining Room. His Sunday after-dinner concerts often featured outstanding vocalists as guest artists.

Across the corridor and up a few steps, the Jasper Tea Room was one of the most unique in Canada, designed by the eminent and sensitive Canadian artist, Edwin Holgate. A contemporary and friend of artist, A.Y. Jackson, his 'Quam, a Chief of the Kitsalas,' and his 'Totem Poles and Gitseguiklas,' among other works, illustrated a popular collection of Indian stories prepared by the well-known Canadian anthropologist, Marius Barbeau.

Merrill Denison wrote in 1929:

"The Jasper Tea Room had no windows. A barrel-vaulted ceiling of bright blue, sown with golden stars, was lit from the upper side of the beams. The dance floor of pegged oak was surrounded by a series of columns carved into totem poles, rich in native symbolism. A terra cotta coloured floor

The elegant main dining room seated 300 guests.

covered the remainder of the room. Paintings of formalized landscapes graced the walls, and opposite the entrance a waterfall splashed into a pool, lit from below by cool green floodlights. On tables that skirted the dance floor were unique lamps whose bases were carved totem poles and whose shades had motifs inspired by the bear, the eagle and the crow. A dado of pegged wood, treated like sea-scoured oak, grey and beautiful, surrounded the room. Subdued lighting created an unworldly twilight that heightened the mysterious forms of half-seen totem poles and other native symbols." [2]

The Jasper Tea Room quickly became a favourite meeting place for Ottawa's young people. They gathered in large numbers at the Saturday afternoon tea dances. Robert Goyette, a Château waiter, remembered:

"For $1.00 patrons were served assorted sandwiches, small tea cakes, coffee or tea. Fashion shows were included in the price, once a month, when R.J. Devlin Furriers and A.J. Freiman Ltd., a leading department store, presented their latest fashions to the music of James McIntyre or Joe de Courcy." [3]

A time when the dollar went further.

Past the Jasper Tea Room and Main Dining Room, five broad carpeted steps led to the entrance of several exquisite rooms. The first of these was the Ball-room Lobby, an imposing room with columns of cream marble supporting the vaulted and decorative ceilings. From here guests moved to the Drawing Room, a large, formal reception room distinguished by wall panels of plaster painted in old ivory. Its rectangular shape was broken at the four corners by detached pillars which created niches in the room. Delicately proportioned mirrors hung on the walls between the columns. Many splendid receptions, such as the one held for General Charles de Gaulle during one of his early visits to Canada, have been held in the Drawing Room.

On the north side of the main floor, overlooking the park, was the Ballroom, a magnificent space with seating capacity for fifteen hundred people. Three mighty chandeliers of frosty crystal provided the main lighting. Hotel staff often watched unobtrusively from behind curtains on the mezzanine when some glittering function was in progress. One such occasion was the State banquet held in 1939 for Their Majesties, King George VI and Queen Elizabeth.

Doors at the east end of the Ballroom opened into the lobby and, at the west end, into the Banquet Room, the old Dining Room in the original building. In 1932 with Prime Minister R.B. Bennett acting as host, the Canadian government held a dinner in honour of Their Majesties, the King and Queen of Siam. The Banquet Room was adorned with a profusion of summer flowers. Brightly coloured uniforms and dainty summer gowns added richness to the setting. His Excellency, the Governor General of Canada, Baron Tweedsmuir, the Siamese staff who accompanied the royal couple to Canada, members of the diplomatic corps, and Cabinet Ministers with their wives, attended the gala evening.

Another outstanding event that year was a Government dinner hosted by Prime Minister Bennett in honour of Earl Jellicoe, the famous British naval officer and Commander of the Battle of Jutland during World War I. Jellicoe was a guest at the Château during his three-day visit to Ottawa.

The Grill Room and Cafeteria

On another level, space in the basement was used to its best advantage. The Grill Room, located behind black, iron grille doors of Spanish design, was air-conditioned long before other establishments knew such luxury. Even on the hottest of Ottawa's well-known sweltering summer days, the Grill was an oasis of coolness. Modelled after an English tap room with walls of pegged-oak planks and low, beamed ceilings, it was a cozy room, a favourite haunt of Members of Parliament, Senators and business people. As well, many Ottawans have celebrated their joyful family occasions at the Grill.

Some people have dined there so often they are allowed to select their own table and waiter. F.M. Ross, a businessman from Vancouver, lived in the Château during World War II. Later, Mr. Ross was appointed Lieutenant Governor of British Columbia and married Mrs. Phyllis Turner, who is the Right Honourable John Turner's mother. Mr. Ross always sat at table 93 in the Grill Room, with Lucien as his waiter. Mayor Charlotte Whitton of Ottawa insisted on sitting at table 95, attended by Clovis Leblanc. She would have no other! Mr. Aylett, long-time hotel Manager, from 1936 until 1957, and his wife had dinner in the Grill almost every evening. If they were by themselves they sat at table 84. If they had guests they chose a large round table, number 72. Mr. Robert Sommerville, General Manager of C.N. Hotels in the 1940's, and his wife preferred to be served by either Tony Popyck or Bill Lacosta.

As well as all the tables surrounding the dance floor, with the orchestra space at the far end of the room, there were deep alcoves set under each

The stylish Canadian Grill quickly proved a popular feature of the 1929 addition.

window. Here refectory tables accommodated from two to six people seated on leather banquettes against the wall.

Tony Popyck, who joined the Château staff in 1929, recalled:

> "The first job they gave me to do was to help move dishes and furniture from the original Grill room to the new Canadian Grill. Then I was sent to the kitchen to be a dishwasher. I'm a Ukrainian who spoke very little English then. After a while, I went to Mr. Helders, Maître d' of the Grill, and asked if I could work there as a bus-boy. 'I can't hire you,' Mr. Helders said. 'As you work in the kitchen, I can't take you from that staff'." [4]

Tony went to the boss in the kitchen and said, "I'm quitting." Which he did. He then returned to Mr. Helders and told him he didn't work in the kitchen any longer, so Mr. Helders hired him.

At first Tony found Mr. Helders to be very strict, but as time went on he appreciated what he learned from him. Before a year was up Mr. Helders wanted to make Tony a waiter, but Popyck did not feel ready as his mastery of English, both spoken and written, was still limited.

"Mr Helders produced a menu and asked me to read it. 'Take my order,' Mr. Helders said. I did that and then the Maître d' said, 'I'll give you two weeks to learn to read the menus and take orders.'

I took a copy of each menu home with me and practised reading them and writing out the orders. Two weeks later, Mr. Helders gave me a slip to present to the stores for a uniform and told me I was now a waiter's apprentice. In another two weeks I was given two tables to wait on at noon each day." [5]

A second basement restaurant, the Cafeteria, was as popular as the Grill Room. In 1963 the management replaced it with a seventeenth-century French-style inn called L'Auberge. Bruce West of the *Globe and Mail* best described the feelings of the patrons at that time:

"Having been a customer for many years at this eating place in the Château's basement, I can say without reservation that, in my opinion, it has always been the ugliest restaurant with the best food in Canada. In appearance it has always resembled nothing so much as a giant gentlemen's powder room, with its tile walls and floors, and its abominable acoustics which takes the rattle of every piece of heavy crockery and multiplies it by several hundred decibels.

But a new customer soon forgot the dismal appearance of the Château's cafeteria when he picked up a tray and started moving along the great serving counter. Behind the steaming and savoury food he would find either Joe Kingsley or Louis Boucher, ready to carve him a slice of roast beef that makes me drool right now to think of it. Both of these jolly chefs have been there for years and years, as have a good many of the Château Laurier's other employees. When you became a regular customer, these gentlemen developed a way of gauging your appetite the moment you pushed up your tray. They could just take a look at you, and tell whether you were in the mood for a thick slice or a thin one, rare, medium, or well done." [6]

The two chefs had a soft spot for the ladies too, and recommended chicken pot pie to them on Thursdays. An aromatic filling of cream sauce, mushrooms, tiny pearl onions, carrots and chicken chunks was nestled under a layer of flaky pastry. That pie was the best seller of any item on any Château menu over the years. Delicate fish dishes were relished, while soups and crusty rolls were a meal in themselves. Luscious fruit pies added just the right touch to end a meal. In the thirties, a meal in the cafeteria would cost a dollar, or a dollar and a quarter. The restaurant was rarely empty, as people could come and go from early morning until eight p.m. Midmorning coffee with bran or corn muffins satisfied the 'no-breakfast' crowd, and shoppers enjoyed fancy desserts with a cup of tea in the afternoon.

At Home On the Mezzanine

On the mezzanine, executive offices, board rooms, convention salons and the catering department were all housed. The Rotary Club had its offices there as well. They had been located in the older section of the hotel since 1916.

As members of a social organizaton, Rotarians are dedicated to the service of less fortunate people, especially handicapped children. Rotarians got their name from their practice in the early days of rotating meetings among members' business establishments. That idea was scrapped later as being impractical. They held their first regular Monday luncheon meeting in the Château on March 20, 1916. Fifty members were present. By 1929, because of

The Château has been the meeting-place of the Rotary Club of Ottawa since 1916.

a growing membership, permanent residence was sought at the hotel. They came to an agreement with the management to rent an office from 1930 until 1952. After this time, the space was needed by the hotel, so the Rotary Club was moved to the basement. By 1965, they were moved back to the mezzanine into Salon 'A'.

At first Rotarians held their luncheons in the Ladies' Café, a small, private dining room. When they outgrew that they were allowed to use the Main Dining Room, provided they guaranteed one hundred and twenty-five members would be present at each luncheon. Luncheon prices in 1930 were one dollar and in 1981, six dollars and fifty cents.

Members of the Rotary Club tried to assist people in need during the Depression. One day during the summer of 1932, Ottawa Rotary President, Bob Stead was attracted by a man playing a violin on an Ottawa street corner. He played exceptionally well, unlike an ordinary street fiddler. Bob bought the man a new shirt, took him to the Rotary Club luncheon at the Château and arranged for him to play for the members. They were impressed. A hat was passed and a happy musician, temporarily down on his luck, left the Château and the city with more than one hundred dollars in his pocket.[7]

Distinctive Suites

Merrill Denison, in the *Canadian National Magazine*, described areas of entertainment:

> "Public and semi-public spaces are by no means restricted to the main floors. On the first floor is the Quebec Suite, installed to take care of private dances, dinners, and functions of from 75 to 125 people. It is a series of connecting rooms arranged with extreme flexibility, quite apart from the public rooms. The host who entertains on a generous scale finds here the living rooms of a sumptuous private home within the confines of a great public hostelry.
>
> An entrance hall gives into a large dining room, and to smaller card and reception rooms. The floors are of parquet hardwood and the decorative scheme throughout is an adaptation of Louis XIV, which creates a distinctly Quebec atmosphere."[8]

Occasionally, when several receptions were scheduled at the same time, a mix-up was bound to happen. Shortly after the Second World War, a wedding reception was held in one of the Château salons for a returning serviceman and his bride. The young lady's mother had saved her sugar and butter rations, which were still in short supply, in order to make the wedding cake. She decorated it with love and great care. When the time came for the bride and groom to cut the cake, they discovered it was not their own. It turned out that their cake had been delivered by mistake to another wedding reception in the Quebec Suite, where the guests had already eaten most of it.

Merrill Denison continued:

"On the sleeping floors above are a number of private suites, all decorated gems and acmes of convenience. These again are for entertaining, on a smaller scale, and each duplicates the living rooms in homes of persons with means, taste and imagination. A number of these suites are located at the south east corner of the building and are known as the Adam, Wren, Regent and Tudor. Each has its own living room, dining room, foyer, bathroom and pantry in which there are a stove, refrigerator and cupboards. Each of the suites is almost a museum piece in the perfection with which the detail of the period has been carried out.

Another interesting suite is the Rideau, located at the north end of the new east wing. It is substantially the same as the others in arrangement, although containing more bedrooms. It is notable for the glorious view of the distant Gatineau Hills and the reaches of the Ottawa River above the Chaudiere Falls, to be seen from its windows. In later years this suite became the official residence of successive Greek ambassadors."

The Chef's Domain

The kitchens, which are of vital importance to any hotel, have been left to the last to describe. Freight entrances to the basement were reached by a low-level roadway on Sussex Street approached through a tunnel under Mackenzie Avenue. Horse-drawn wagons backed into the tunnel as there was no place for them to turn around. Kitchen employees entered the Château by this route also.

Cleanliness and coolness were the most notable characteristics of the kitchens. Even the space in front of the gas ranges was kept reasonably cool through perfectly installed ventilation. Mr. Van Wyck and the architects had utilized the space with great efficiency. There were no columns, pipes or ducts to cut up the kitchen and hinder good lighting. The white tiled walls gleamed. Van Wyck was insistent that the kitchens and the food should be the finest possible, "...as any hotel is only as good as the food served therein." [9]

Areas for baking, butchering and salad preparation were kept scrupulously clean. Scores of refrigerators lined the walls of the main kitchen and corridors.

All the ice required for the hotel was manufactured in a large ice plant in the sub-basement. A power plant in Union Station supplied electricity to the Château through a service tunnel between the two buildings.

Carlos Scarabelli was a superb master chef. Born in Milan, Italy, he had worked in several cities in Europe before going to London, England. There he served at the Savoy and Claridges and then on to the Ritz Carlton in New York. At the age of forty, he arrived at the Château Laurier from Jasper Park Lodge.

Scarabelli was quoted as saying, "The foundation of all good cooking is French. One may vary the details, but always they are merely new ideas superimposed upon a French foundation." [10] Chef Scarabelli thought Canadians should eat more lamb and he considered Canadian lamb to be the best in the world. It was not uncommon to find lamb featured on the menu.

A later master chef, Henri Freitag, was renowned for his culinary talent in Switzerland before coming to Canada. When the King and Queen were en route back to England from Canada in 1939, Freitag was summoned from the Château to prepare their food at the Nova Scotian Hotel in Halifax.

Edna Inglis, writing in the *Canadian National Magazine* in 1931, recalled:

"In addition to the à-la-carte menu with its daily specials in each course, the chef prepares a table d'hôte dinner, served in the Main Dining Room and the Grill Room. At noon, a special Ladies' luncheon is served in the Main Dining room, and a Business Men's lunch is served in the Grill Room. Menus are always prepared twenty-four hours ahead and foods in season are featured. Every day the chef knows how many meals will be served.

Ottawa residents who frequented the Château knew that on a certain day of the week they were almost sure to find a particularly favourite dish on the menu. The chicken pot pie was the main reason the Grill Room was full to overflowing at noon on Thursdays. On Mondays onion soup was especially good; on Tuesdays a hamburger steak or oxtail soup; on Wednesdays finnan haddie cooked in the chef's inimitable way; on Friday filet of sole, and on Saturday the chef roasted a whole leg of beef. Usually prize beef was available and it looked most appetizing roasting on a spit."

The new Château Laurier of 1929 had become as Merrill Denison expressed it *The Complete Hotel*. From décor, to the most modern and conveniently laid-out facilities, to the best food and service in Ottawa, the Château had no equal.

Chapter Five

IT WAS THE WORST OF TIMES, IT WAS THE BEST OF TIMES

W*HEN 1929 BEGAN PEOPLE WERE ENJOYING LIFE.* The western world had been full of exhuberance all through the 1920's. As popular as the Château Laurier had been before the new construction took place, its fame spread even further after the rebuilding was completed. The hotel was constantly busy. Luncheons, dinners, banquets, and conventions were daily occurrences. The interests of groups attending these gatherings were as diverse as their names would indicate, from the Carleton Federation of Agriculture right on through the alphabet to the Victorian Order of Nurses and the Zionist Movement of Canada. Delegates came to conventions from every province in Canada, from Newfoundland, the Yukon and the Northwest Territories. They came from many parts of the United States and from overseas. Everyone spoke in glowing terms of the Château's comfort, service and excellent food.

Then came the 1929 stock crash. The whole industrial world staggered under its impact. Ottawa, as a city, was in bad shape. Business slowed down, and businessmen attempted to carry on in a very restricted manner. Some declared bankruptcy. In order to find ways to stimulate the economy, it was proposed that the city should take advantage of Ottawa's winter climate. Consequently the advantages of Ottawa's winter sports facilities were advertised to the country at large and to the U.S.A. in particular.

During the first week of February, 1930, an International Winter Carnival was staged. An abundance of snow lying on the hills just a few minutes drive north of the city provided the best skiing conditions within a hundred miles. In town, hockey and skating were already well established on outdoor rinks scattered around each ward in the city. Several curling clubs flourished. Skiing and tobogganing on smaller hills in Rockcliffe Park and the Dominion Experimental Farm Aboretum were free and great fun for the young of all ages.

Earlier carnivals, which had begun with the one in 1922, had been organized on a more limited level. Now sled-dog racing, tobogganing, snowshoeing, skiing, skating, hockey, curling and even indoor swimming championships were to take place. The snowshoers met in Ottawa as an International Convention, with races for world championships. The dog derby brought the world's most celebrated mushers to the Capital. Ski races were run for both provincial and international titles, men vied for the Canadian championships in speed skating, and the women competed for the North American title. Swimmers and divers strove for national acclaim at the swimming competitions held in the new Château Laurier pool.

In a week crowded with all these activities, the dog derby was the most outstanding event. The race was to commence and finish in front of the Château, with first prize to be one thousand dollars donated by city merchants. The route had to be covered each day for three successive days and the winner would be the one who covered the total ninety-nine miles in the shortest time.

There were seven entrants in the derby. Emile St. Godard, winner of many dog derbies, came from The Pas, Manitoba. His friend and enthusiastic rival, Earl Bridges, who already held five records, arrived from Cranberry Portage, Manitoba. Leonhard Seppala of Nome, Alaska, who had won a place in history for a dash he made to Nome to pick up serum for diptheria sufferers in remote areas in Alaska, was another contestant. Walter Channing, a highly respected amateur driver and breeder of dogs, came from Boston. Harry Wheeler, who raced for Grey Rocks Inn, St. Jovite, Quebec was another entrant. The youngest man, Georges Chevrette, competed for F. Canac Marquis of Quebec, and Frank Dupuis, a flamboyant driver from Berthier, Quebec, raced for the 'Come-On' Travellers' Club. The only woman entrant, Mrs. E.P. Richer Jr., came from Poland Springs, Maine. However, she was unable to race as her dogs' feet were not in racing condition. Another disappointed musher was Jack Melville of Lac Traverse, Ontario. He drove the Château Laurier dog team all the way from Syracuse, New York to Ottawa, advertising the carnival every step of the way, but arrived just too late to start in the race.

Ottawans forgot about lunch and business for that afternoon. People poured out of government offices and stores and crowded into the square overlooked by the Château and the Post Office. Some of them stayed in their places for four hours so as not to miss the triumphant finish of the race. Exuberant youths climbed onto the top of the canopy over the Château doorway, while others were on the roofs of the Union Station and the Post Office.

The entire course was packed with spectators good naturedly stamping their feet in the snow or hopping up and down and clapping their hands together in an effort to keep warm. Thermos bottles of hot soup were brought along to stave off the chill. In some cases, flasks of something stronger were in evidence. Children were bundled up so tightly, only their eyes and noses were visible. This writer, at eleven years of age, watched with her family along Carling Avenue and was excited enough to 'burst at the seams'.

At exactly twelve noon the dogs and their drivers were off. They tore down the Driveway past the Exhibition grounds and under the Bank Street bridge, on through the Central Experimental Farm, raced west on Carling Avenue to Britannia, then on to Bell's Corners. From there they turned south to Fallowfield, across the county road to the Prescott Highway, and sped back along the same route, with St. Godard in the lead. Brydges and Seppala were only seconds apart, vying with each other for second place. At full speed they reached the finish line at the Château. St. Godard won each day with a total time of eight hours, thirteen minutes and twenty-three seconds. Brydge's aggregate was eight hours, thirty-three minutes and forty-five seconds. Seppala was only twenty-eight seconds behind Brydges.

R.H. Ayre wrote in March, 1930:

> "The dog derby wound up in triumph at a Carnival Ball in the Château Laurier. The arrival of their Excellencies, Governor General, the Viscount Willingdon and Viscountess Willingdon, was announced by a bugle, and Mayor Frank Plant escorted them to a dais at the centre of the ballroom. Mrs. Richer, the woman musher, was Queen of the Ball. All mushers arrived in their picturesque parkas and mocassins. St. Godard, who brought his famous lead dog, 'Toby', was greeted with applause and a salute from the Château Laurier Orchestra as they played, 'See the Conquering Hero Come'. His Excellency congratulated St. Godard, and presented him with the Gold Challenge Cup and a cheque for one thousand dollars. The cup was filled with warm milk for Toby. Then St. Godard and Toby left the hotel for their own celebration." [1]

The revellers carried on with their Ball. Ayre continued:

> "The pace of the carnival was set by several thousand snowshoers who spent Saturday and Sunday, February first and second, in Ottawa. Special

trains brought them from New England and from all parts of Quebec and Ontario. They took the Château Laurier and the city of Ottawa by storm. For two days they made the corridors of the hotel and the streets resound with their shouts and songs, to say nothing of the racket of their bugles and drums, frying pans and tin plates. They were given the freedom of the city in the form of a huge 'gold key' and they made the most of it. After the official welcome at City Hall, they held their world championship snowshoe races, won by Mirth McKecheanneay from Montreal. When that part of the programme was over, the men went off to the Drill Hall for a baked bean supper and the ladies were given a Tea at the Château. An enormous bonfire on Cartier Square, off Elgin Street, ended the Carnival." [2]

The festivities brought people to Ottawa to enjoy themselves and, in turn, added revenue to city businesses. For one week the Carnival gave everyone a feeling of exhilaration and fun. Most Ottawa citizens watched the gaiety and felt the excitement of the dog sled and snowshoe races in a spirit of camaraderie often difficult to find in such troubled times.

Inevitably, such an exuberant crowd would do some damage to the Château Laurier. One of the large Chinese vases at the door of the Main Dining Room was smashed, feathers littered bedrooms where high-spirited guests held pillow fights, and some items went missing from hotel rooms.

When St. Godard won the senior race again the following year, Prime Minister R.B. Bennett presented him with the Gold Challenge Cup outside on the steps of the hotel. Any item which could be battened down for the occasion was secured, and management locked away many fragile items for the duration of the Carnival.

The Bennett Years

Richard Bedford Bennett had become leader of the Federal Conservative Party of Canada at its leadership convention in 1927. A big man who dressed extremely well in a formal way, Bennett was rotund, largely because of his fondness for chocolates which he ate by the box.

As a lawyer, Bennett had good contacts and served a number of prestigious clients, including the Canadian Pacific Railway. Through a series of astute investments he had become a wealthy man. He was first elected to Parliament as Member for Calgary in 1911. After the Château Laurier opened in 1912, he occupied a small suite there whenever the House was in session.

This 1934 photo of Prime Minister R.B. Bennett adorned the menu of a dinner held for the Conservative Members of Parliament.

The Conservatives looked to their new leader to show strong opposition to the then Prime Minister, the Right Honourable William Lyon Mackenzie King, and to win the next election, which he proceeded to do in 1930. Bennett and his party were in power for five of the most difficult years of the Great Depression.

One of Bennett's first personal requirements was more appropriate living accommodation and he considered buying a house in Ottawa. When Sir Henry Thornton, President of Canadian National Railways and Hotels, heard that news, he approached Bennett and asked if he would remain at the Château if a suitable suite of rooms could be arranged for him. Thornton suggested that a number of rooms which were small and difficult to rent could be made into a suite as his official residence. The Prime Minister agreed, providing the cost would not exceed fifty thousand dollars. He said he would pay six per cent of the cost of renovation as rent.

Again the Foundation Company of Canada was given the contract to do the work, supervised by architects, Archibald and Schofield. A portion of the first floor hallway and the small bedrooms on either side of it had to be gutted to form the suite. Replacement of some of the original heating, lighting and plumbing equipment was also necessary because of some deterioration. New pillars needed to be installed to carry the weight of the structures, and the rooms themselves rebuilt. Painting and decorating and furnishings brought the total estimate to $98,398.21.

Bennett was in England when he received word of the cost. He cabled the Acting Deputy Minister of Railways and Canals as follows:

> "Please advise Perley (*Acting Prime Minister, the Hon. Sir George Perley*) I agree that at cost indicated proposed alteration should not be made at Château. In any event had intended paying interest on capital expenditure on Château. Bennett, London, 3 October 1930."[3]

Thornton decided to go ahead anyway as he explained in a letter he wrote on January 2, 1931 to the Honourable R.J. Manion, Minister of Railways and Canals:

> "It means a good deal to have the Prime Minister living at the Château Laurier. It lends prestige to the hotel and indirectly brings to us considerable revenue. Should he ever decide to go elsewhere, there would not be any trouble in renting the space to some one of the foreign diplomats located in Ottawa, or to others. In other words, the accommodation would in no sense be wasted. Yours sincerely, H.W. Thornton."[4]

Word got out in Parliament that the Prime Minister would only be paying four hundred dollars a month for such an elaborate residence. There was a terrible ruckus in the House. The Depression had intensified and thousands of men were out of work and often homeless. Mothers were at their wits' end trying to feed and clothe their families, while the Prime Minister was living in luxury for pennies a day. When asked in Parliament if he thought this fair, Bennett replied that he paid what was asked of him.

The C.N.R. President really felt the whole thing was an internal matter for the railway and could not understand why there was so much opposition. The amount charged directly for the reconstruction suite was reduced to

$85,590.99, as it was felt the cost of repair work and the need for stronger pillars should not be charged to the expense of the suite. Similarly, the cost of the furniture was omitted as Thornton argued it could be used again in another section of the hotel.

Bennett's sister, Mildred Bennett, lived at the Château with her brother and acted as his hostess until her marriage to W.D. Herridge in 1931. A.W. Mirriam was Bennett's private secretary. Miss Alice Millar, who also lived at the Château, was one of his assistants. She and Mildred Bennett got along well together, as this little story illustrates:

> "One day in Ottawa after he (Bennett) became Prime Minister, Mildred came into his suite in the Château Laurier after a shopping expedition and incautiously told her brother she had bought a new hat, and how much it cost. It provoked one of his sudden bursts of temper to which Mildred listened patiently. After he had gone, she turned to Alice Millar and said: 'Millar (she always used her surname), don't ever walk out on Dick. We're the bumpers on his car. We save him a lot of damage'." [5]

An Ottawa lawyer, Ross Tolmie recalled:

> "Bennett decided things for himself and God help any Minister who disagreed with him. There is an old story about an American tourist who saw a man in a swallow-tailed coat, walking along Wellington Street from the Parliament Buildings to the Château, mumbling to himself as he went. 'Who is that man?', the tourist asked of an Ottawa citizen. 'That's R.B. Bennett, our Prime Minister.' 'Why is he talking to himself?' the tourist wanted to know. 'He's not talking to himself. He's holding a Cabinet Meeting,' was the reply." [6]

Edith Lancaster remembered:

> "Mr. Bennett often came to the office to see Mr. Van Wyck. I frequently met him on the stairway, as our office was on the mezzanine, and he usually walked down the stairs from his suite on his way to the House of Commons. When I was ill in the hospital in 1935, Mr. Bennett not only sent me flowers, but on my return to the office he came to see me and, with his rare smile, said, 'We missed you and are glad to have you back running the hotel.'
>
> State dinners at which Mr. Bennett was host were held in the Ballroom, with receptions in the Drawing Room. Mildred Bennett's wedding dinner was held in the Ballroom, and the reception preceding it in the Drawing

Room. The floral decorations were beautiful. They were all arranged by the hotel florist and supervised by the Catering Manager, Mr. John Adam, who was very artistic."[7]

Henri Seguin, one of the staff on duty at that wedding, recalls seeing the Prime Minister's wedding gift to Mildred and her husband. According to Henri, it was a cheque, placed across her plate at the dinner table, believed to be in excess of one million dollars.[8]

During Bennett's regime there were State dinners given for several illustrious visitors. Among them were Their Royal Highnesses, the Prince and Princess Takamatsu of Japan. They stayed at the Château for four or five days while in Canada on their honeymoon. Cherry blossoms and numerous other delightful spring flowers were used profusely throughout the Ballroom suite when the Prime Minister hosted a dinner for the young couple. The Prince and Princess were also invited to dine in the Quebec Suite by the Japanese Minister to Canada, the Hon. I. Tokuwaga. After that dinner, five hundred guests gathered in the Drawing Room to be presented to Their Royal Highnesses.

Roger de Repentigny, Bellman; Andy Abbott, Bell Captain; Henri Seguin, Bellman.

Money Problems

Henri Seguin, who began working at the Château as a lad of fourteen in 1928, described:

> "For the first three months I worked without pay in order to learn English. Part of the time during the Depression three floors were closed at the hotel for lack of business. There were twenty-five of us bellboys. Our salary fell to ten dollars a month plus tips. Some days the Bell Captain would ask, 'Who wants to go home?' No one wanted to go home as they wouldn't be paid."

Several of these young men played musical instruments. They made extra money by moonlighting with various bands around the Ottawa area. One evening a lady asked Henri to play a song 'Souvenirs' for her. He did and she kept requesting it all evening. Each time he played she gave him a dollar. "I would have been willing to play the same piece all night for her." [9]

Sir Henry Thornton responded to the Depression by cutting out railway luxuries and trimming salaries of both railway and hotel employees. He refused to make drastic cuts in staff because he said, "You cannot turn people loose and merely transfer the burden of their maintenance from the railway to the government." [10] He respected the employees, and they in turn admired him.

During these difficult times, Thornton became a scapegoat for all C.N. errors and omissions, real or imagined. Several conservative members of the Commons Railway Committee criticized him for spending so much on the Prime Minister's suite in the Château Laurier and on his own house in Montreal. They accused the C.N. of corruption and extravagance. Thornton refused to reply and on July 19, 1932 he resigned. Rail employees felt they had lost a friend.

Chapter Six

EYES OF THE EMPIRE
ON THE CHÂTEAU

THE FIRST IMPERIAL ECONOMIC CONFERENCE to be held outside London, England, took place in Ottawa in 1932. The other unique feature of this Conference was that it lasted for a whole month. In England, each delegation would be housed in a separate hotel, however in Ottawa, all the delegates, wives and entourage were housed at the Château Laurier. Many of the Château's meeting rooms were also used for informal gatherings of the delegates. Months of planning went into this event to assure its success. The Government Hospitality Committee worked closely with Walter Pratt, Head of C.N. Hotel Department and Joseph Van Wyck, Manager of the Château.

Edith Lancaster, then working in Mr. Van Wyck's office, recalled:

> "We had to clear out the hotel. Days before the Conference began, no new guests were accepted at the Château as others checked out. Only the permanent guests, including Prime Minister Bennett, were allowed to stay." [1]

Danny Lupino remembered:

> "All the staff who were on part-time or laid off until the Depression ended were called in to work full-time while the Conference was in session. I was able to save thirty-five dollars that month and thought I was rich." [2]

From the Château Mr. Van Wyck sent Harold Morgan, one of his Assistant Managers, and Albert Hunt, his Head Porter, to Pointe au Père, Quebec on the south shore of the St. Lawrence. There they met the British delegation arriving on board the luxury liner, Empress of Britain. The two men boarded the ship along with the river pilots who had guided the great vessel up the river to the docks at Wolfe's Cove, a mile upstream from Quebec City. Morgan and Hunt registered all the guests entraining for Ottawa while they were still on board the Empress. The baggage was numbered, transferred to the boat-train for Ottawa and safely delivered to the guests' rooms without a single piece going astray.

Union Station was thronged with cheering Ottawa citizens as Prime Minister Bennett and other government officials awaited the arrival of the train on the morning of Tuesday, July 19. There were warm hellos, handshakes and back-slapping when the visitors came through the concourse gates. Many of these prominent men had met on previous occasions. Other delegates to the Convention arrived via Montreal, New York and Vancouver and received the same kind of attention.

An article written in August, entitled 'Housing the Empire's Statesmen', described the scene at the Château after all the delegates had arrived:

> "Never in the history of the Château Laurier have its lobbies and corridors presented such a colourful appearance, as when delegates from India, in characteristic garb, paused to exchange pleasantries with others from New Zealand or Australia or Ireland. Secretaries, assistants and stenographers from Britain, Ireland or elsewhere paused in their work to marvel at the class of service and accommodation found in Canadian hotels and trains, so different from what they had anticipated when they left home prepared, if necessary, 'to rough it a bit'." [3]

All the usual services were available to make the guests comfortable. Added perks were early morning tea, mail delivery to the suites and a shoeshine service.

At the time of the Conference, the newly opened Therapeutic and Swimming Pool Department, in the east wing of the hotel, were made available to the visitors. The health facility, modelled on famous European spas, was the most complete and up-to-date in North America. The first director, Dr. Ball, had over twenty-five years of experience in Europe.

A gymnasium held all the well-known equipment of a modern health club. An adjoining room served for massage and infra-red lamp treatments for certain kidney and bladder troubles. A super-alpine-model ultra-violet ray lamp helped people with rickets or those who suffered from poliomyelitis. Small growths and warts were treated with high-frequency platinum instruments brought to a white heat. A high-frequency current also developed heat in deep tissues and joints of the body, and was used for relief of rheumatism, sciatica, high blood pressure and many other diseases.

One amazing room had walls and ceilings completely lined with aluminum. Scotch douche treatments given there consisted of spraying the spine of a patient with alternate streams of hot and cold water sprays, and showers. It was considered to be one of the most uniquely equipped room of its kind in the world. A steam blanket was part of the equipment for wrapping patients warmly after their treatments.

Hydro therapy for chronic rheumatism, stiffness and pain after injury, and electric therapy for certain nervous afflictions were other programmes offered. High blood pressure was treated on a special electrically constructed table known as a Nagleschmidt couch. Sprays for nose and throat with hot and cold condensed air were available. Hanoria Alpine sun apparatus suspended from the ceiling and positioned over treatment couches gave off ultra-violet rays. One room contained a Nauheim carbonic acid bath. This treatment was given exactly as it was done in Neinheim, Germany and had been used successfully in enlarged-heart conditions.

The crowning jewel of the whole department was the new Art Deco swimming pool, sixty feet long by twenty-five feet wide and nine feet at the deep end. The emerald clear water was constantly changed, regulated to any desired

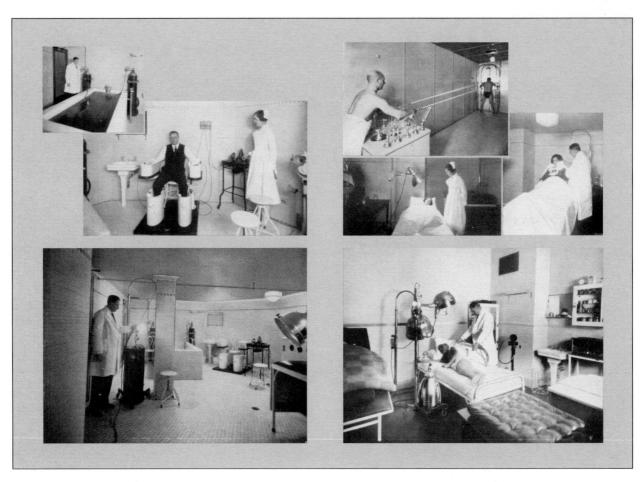

These layouts from a 1931 Château Laurier promotional booklet describe the various treatments and pieces of special equipment that were available in the Hydro- and Electro-Therapeutic Department. Photographs on the left portray the Nauheim and Schnee Baths and on the right, the Scotch Douche.

temperature and chemically treated. Sponge rubber covered the floor on either side of the pool. One side was left unfurnished so that patrons could walk about, while the opposite was comfortably furnished with potted palms, rattan chairs and sun lamps. The walls of the pool room were of pale pink Tennessee marble with dark green Arizona-marble pillars at either end.

An intricately carved hand-wrought railing surrounded the gallery and beneath it hung twelve imported sun-ray lamps. The far end of the room was fashioned in the same marble and contained an alcove filled with fresh green plants. The whole effect gave the feeling of a tropical resort. Turkish baths, change rooms and rest rooms completed this section of the hotel. Imperial Conference delegates were amazed to find such facilities at the Château Laurier.

As described in the 1931 promotion booklet 'the beautiful pool offers the luxury of a plunge in the greenish-blue opalescent waters of a tropical sea'. Left, the pool and its bordering Palm-decked lounge. The Lounge is shown above right, a more detailed photograph of the Gallery appears below.

The Therapeutic Department was in use until after World War II and then disbanded. As more hospitals became involved in therapeutic treatments and as commercial health centres began to emerge, the department lost its public appeal.

The swimming pool is still as popular as ever, not only with hotel guests but numerous Ottawa residents as well. Many Ottawa children, including former Ottawa Mayor, Marion Dewar, learned to swim there. The former Governor General Roland Michener and the Hon. George Hees, retired Minister of Veterans' Affairs, and other notables enjoy a daily swim at the Château whenever they are in Ottawa.

The Conference opened with great pomp and pageantry on Thursday morning, July 21. A huge crowd filled the square in front of the Parliament Buildings. Promptly at 10:40 a.m. the Governor General's Foot Guards Band announced the arrival of the guard of honour. In spite of the heat, the Guardsmen wore their bearskin hats and scarlet uniforms with gold facing. Carillon music pealed out from the Peace Tower. Precisely at 10:55 a.m. a mounted detachment of Dragoons, with pennants flapping in the breeze and with their shiny brass helmets glittering in the sun, preceded His Excellency, the Governor General, the Earl of Bessborough, riding in a coach and four from Government House. Two postilions in scarlet uniforms were mounted on the front horses, while two footmen rode perched on seats at the rear of the carriage. A second detachment of Dragoons brought up the rear.

The House of Commons witnessed its most illustrious gathering to date. Conference delegates were all seated in the floor of the House, while Members of Parliament and Senators occupied seats in the Gallery along with their wives and the Press. A message from King George V was read by the Governor General, after which he welcomed all the Commonwealth visitors. The Rt. Hon. Stanley Baldwin rose to propose that Prime Minister Bennett be elected

A grand occasion in the Ballroom, 1933.

as Chairman of the Conference, a proposal unanimously adopted. The Conference was underway.

That same evening the Government of Canada entertained seven hundred guests at a State dinner in the Ballroom of the Château Laurier. All the delegates to the Conference, Canadian Members of Parliament and Senators, leaders of the provincial governments and members of the Privy Council and their wives were in attendance.

The scene was memorable. Down the east side of the vast room, the long head table was dressed in green damask and adorned with a lavish display of Château Laurier Limoges china in creamy white with a royal blue and gold border bearing the hotel crest. Silver candelabra, lighted tapers and brilliant summer flowers completed the elaborate display. Prime Minister Bennett sat at the centre of the table. On the wall behind him hung flags of all the Commonwealth countries. Eleven shorter tables fanned out from the main table and seated most of the other guests. The overflow sat in the alcoves on the mezzanine floor overlooking the Ballroom.

The men wore formal evening dress. The ladies were dressed in spectacular gowns reflecting the fashions of their heritage. Mrs. Stanley Baldwin wore a handsome gown of yellow brocade, embroidered with topaz beads, and shoes of the same tone. A pearl necklace completed her attire. Mrs. Haroon of India was dressed in a white sari, handpainted with rose and dusted with gold and silver. Her jewellery consisted of diamond earrings, necklace and bangles. Her shoes were gold and black.

Speeches, which did not start until after ten o'clock, were brief. The Prime Minister spoke first and referred to the dinner as a 'family gathering'. He pointed out the fact that there were, among the guests, three former Prime Ministers, a former Lord Chancellor of Great Britain, a present Chancellor of the Exchequer, and that the Premier of Southern Rhodesia was a nephew of the great missionary, Stanley Livingstone. The Prime Minister then offered a toast to 'our guests'.

The Rt. Hon. Stanley Baldwin then rose and thanked Prime Minister Bennett for the way in which the delegates had been received on arrival by members of the Government and by the Château staff. "Everything has been done for our comfort," he said. All the other delegates expressed similar words of appreciation.[4]

Mrs. Baldwin also spoke at that dinner. She recalled a previous visit to Canada with her husband and remarked, "One thing I carry in my memory happened one night, five years ago, in Winnipeg. My husband spoke from a verandah. I shall never forget those upturned faces as a band played 'Oh Canada'. The memory of that has never left me. I hope before I leave, I shall hear that song again." With that, Prime Minister Bennett stood up and motioned to the orchestra. Everyone rose and sang 'Oh Canada,' some in English, some in French. It was a most successful evening." [5]

The Château was a hub of activity with, it seemed, the Empire coming and going hourly. Everyone was affected. When asked, "Are the delegates easier on the furniture than the snowshoers?" Mr. Van Wyck replied, "Yes, indeed they are." The page boys had some tongue-twister names to call out during the Conference. One of them remarked, "Suppose I had to call out, 'Sir Abul C. Chatterjie, Sir Paramji Pestonji Ginevala, and Seth Haji Haroon' all at once?" [6]

Recalling this time, Edith Lancaster said:

> "I frequently met Mr. Baldwin on the stairway. He was going out early. I was going up to our offices on the mezzanine. He was very courteous, saying, 'How are you, my girl; pretty busy these days?'. I also saw his wife. She was old-fashioned looking, always wearing a hat out of which one expected a bird to fly." [7]

Even the Churches took an interest in the Conference proceedings. A day of prayer for the success of the Conference was set by the Federal Government for Sunday, July 24. On weekends during the Conference everyone relaxed. Some heads of delegations attended semi-official dinners at the Royal Ottawa Golf Club and the Ottawa Hunt and Golf Club. Many were invited by the Canadians to their homes or summer cottages.

While the men were at their business sessions during the week, the wives were entertained almost daily by Ottawa society ladies. In return, the British wives gave a series of three afternoon teas, each a week apart, held in the Drawing room at the Château. Mrs. Stanley Baldwin, Mrs. J.H. Thomas, Viscountess Hailsham and Mrs. Runciman were the hostesses on each of these occasions. The gatherings were meant as a means for all visiting ladies to become acquainted with Canadian women. Over one hundred ladies attended each of the receptions, all dressed in their fashionable summer afternoon gowns.

Britain had set up the Conference with high hopes of securing a common market with the Dominions. Each hot July day as the Conference progressed and the British agenda did not, Bennett became more difficult. Furiously, he attempted to impose his will on the men who ran the Empire. The M.P. spokesman with the press, R.J. Manion, gave Canadian journalists scarcely any news, while Lord Runciman and Sir Neville Chamberlain reported to the British Press each evening in the Château. Eventually, after difficult negotiations, the deadlock was broken and the Conference closed with an Anglo-Canadian trade pact.

Two more social events worthy of mention took place at the Château before the Conference adjourned. At one, the Corporation of the City of Ottawa hosted a luncheon to honour the Conference delegates on August 17. One hundred and fifty guests attended with His Worship, Mayor J.J. Allen presiding.

The other was held on August 18 when the Lord President of the Council, the Rt. Hon. Stanley Baldwin, hosted, on behalf of the whole British delegation, one of the most memorable evenings in the history of the Château Laurier. The eighteen hundred guests who filled the Ballroom included all the delegates of each country, the technical advisers, members of the Canadian Cabinet, the Senate, the House of Commons, the Diplomatic Corps, the Press and those Ottawa residents who had entertained the visitors during their stay in the city. Many were accompanied by their wives and families. It was the first opportunity the United Kingdom group had to show their appreciation to the Canadians.

Mrs. Baldwin was in a striking gown of black and silver lamé, shot with prismatic colours, gracefully draped and touching the floor. She wore a diamond tiara, long pearl necklace, silver and black shoes, and carried a pearl-handled feather fan. The Baldwins greeted their guests in the Drawing Room. In the Ballroom, the walls were hung with Union Jacks and the flags of the other Dominions, each adding more colour to the already brilliant scene. In the East Wing, an abundance of fresh summer flowers adorned all the public rooms. Music for dancing was provided by the Château Laurier Orchestra.

The guests found supper laid out on a long buffet table in the Main Dining Room. They sat in that room or in the Jasper Room. It was a typical English supper of large joints of roast beef, saddles of mutton and crowns of lamb, as well as assorted hors d'oeuvres, salads, chicken in aspic and Virginia hams. The sweet course consisted of a number of large cakes, a fitting conclusion to this noteworthy Imperial Economic Conference. The Conference formally closed during a ceremony in the House of Commons on Saturday morning, August 20, 1932.

Shortly after the visitors arrived home, the C.N. Hotel Department received numerous letters of praise for Ottawa and the Château Laurier. Mr. Baldwin wrote a personal letter to Mr. Van Wyck, acknowledging "the efficiency and unfailing courtesy which we have received at your hands during the Conference." J.F. Murphy, Secretary of the Australian group, wrote: "One of the outstanding impressions of our busy sojourn in Ottawa will always be your excellent organization and the comfort of the luxurious Château." Mr. Moffat of the Southern Rhodesia party said, "My colleagues retain memories of the very pleasant time spent at the Château during the month." [8]

The Château Laurier had become more entrenched than ever in the political and social life of the Capital.

VIGNETTES OF
THE THIRTIES

A LONG WITH HIS STRONG PERSONALITY and a dedication to his work, Van Wyck had the ability to choose outstanding people for his staff. In 1934 he became General Manager of all the Canadian National Hotels and moved their Head Office to Ottawa into the new east wing of the Château. "So much of the Château Laurier's business is with the government here that I should remain in the Capital where I am most needed."[1]

The man Van Wyck wanted for the Château Laurier on a long-term basis was an Englishman, William Aylett. Eventually Van Wyck enticed him away from the Windsor Hotel in Montreal, while the Canadian Pacific Hotels' General Manager was off in Europe. Aylett's first assignment took him to the Macdonald Hotel in Edmonton for a year to gain some experience in the operation of C.N. Hotels. In December 1935, he arrived in Ottawa to take over as Manager of the Château Laurier, replacing interim manager, Robert Pitt, who was transferred to the Nova Scotian Hotel in Halifax.

Big Bill Aylett, as he became known during his tenure, remained as Château Manager for twenty-one years, host to one and all. Six foot four inches tall, broad shouldered, with dark hair and brown eyes, Mr. Aylett was a man who commanded respect.

Very much a gentleman, he was a bit reserved, but eager to receive his guests with a smile. He made it a routine to stand in the lobby each day at noon and again late in the afternoon when he greeted his guests. A fastidious dresser, Aylett always looked immaculate. He possessed a fair sense of humour, although he seldom relaxed with employees. There is a story about him going on holiday one year. He said good-bye to his staff, who expected he would be gone the next day. They couldn't believe their eyes in the morning when they went into the office and found Aylett there, unshaven and in his shirt sleeves. There had been a fire in the electrical system during the night and the manager never did get to bed.

Mr. and Mrs. Aylett occupied a two-room suite on the fifth floor of the hotel during his entire tenure at the Château Laurier. Often they had dinner in the Canadian Grill. On those occasions when they preferred the privacy of their suite, Mr. Aylett ordered from Room Service. When a waiter arrived at their door and knocked, someone would call, "Come in," but there was never anyone in the sitting-room. When the waiter returned, the trolley would be ready for him with an invariable fifty-cent tip on the tray. Still no one would be in sight!

Bill Aylett's hotel experience came from the Hurlingham Club in England and the Château Frontenac in Quebec City. After a stint in the British army during World War I, he had returned to Canada to join the Ritz Carlton and later the Windsor Hotel in Montreal.

William Aylett, Château Manager from 1935 to 1957.

Occasionally, a person could make Aylett lose his patience. Once the staff was upset with a man who rated as somebody in his home town and expected similar treatment away from home. Aylett let him know, without raising his voice, that the staff had failed to realize his importance because he shouted so much, a thing most important people did not do. The man continued to stay at the Château, but was noticeably less vocal.

Another story was told of a man who decided to commit suicide. He checked out of the Château and into a lesser hotel so as not to arouse Aylett's anger. Always a man of discretion, the Manager would not confirm this story. Nor would he confirm another which says Mr. Aylett went to a party in Ottawa at which he was served a drink from a tray he recognized as belonging to the hotel. He calmly asked the hostess to wrap up the tray so that he could take it with him when he left. [2]

McKenzie Porter, writing in 1954, remarked:

> "Aylett has the toughest hotel job in Canada. He works for the C.N.R. which owns the Château, but as Manager of the Château he is a semi-official host for the government, which controls the C.N.R. The government expects him to operate the Château lavishly and graciously. The C.N.R. expects him to keep the government happy without losing money — this is a hotel planned more for show than for profit. The C.N.R. also expects him to avoid charging rates that will bring noisy parliamentary protests from guests who are also M.P.'s and Senators." [3]

Music at the Château

Musicians have always been an important element of the hotel staff. From concert orchestras with featured instrumentalists and guest soloists to local bands, music has been a part of the life and ambience of the hotel.

One musician, Ozzie Williams, remembers:

> "Mr. Pitt hired my band of eleven members. We came from Guelph, Ontario. I was maestro in the Canadian Grille from the autumn of 1936 until the spring of 1938. Two bands which played at the Château before us were those of Joe de Courcy, followed by Gene Fogarty. Len Hopkins arrived after we left. The first year, we broadcast on radio regularly over the Canadian Radio Commission station CRCO from the Château. It later became the CBC. Some of our announcers were Herb May, Syd Brown, Alan McFee and Ted Briggs." [4]

Len Hopkins auditioned for Mr. Aylett in a room over a Chinese Restaurant in London, Ontario in 1938. He was then offered a week's trial at the Château Laurier, where he remained playing in the Canadian Grill until 1956.

> "Like Guy Lombardo, Hopkins is a native of London, Ontario and plays slow, sweet, rhythmic music. He is forever being asked to play *Tea for Two*, *Rose Marie*, *Ramona*, *Valencia* and other favourites of the past. In the summer, he transfers his band to the C.N.R.'s Jasper Park Lodge in Alberta. There, recently, two guests named Bing Crosby and Dinah Shore liked his music so much, they got up and sang with him." [5]

Len Hopkins.

Sylvia Margosches Haltrecht remembers when she was about fourteen, she and her girlfriend, Rosalind Gluck Barrett, were roaming around the Château one day while waiting for Sylvia's mother. Mrs. Margosches was attending a meeting of the Lord Reading Cultural Club in the hotel.

As the two young girls walked along the corridor leading to the Ballroom, they heard music, and peeked in the open door. There sat two men, one playing the piano, the other a cello. On noticing the girls, the men beckoned them into the room but stopped playing, a disappointment to Sylvia and Rosalind. The musicians wanted to know why the girls were in the hotel and chatted with them. The cellist was a famous New York musician, Gregor Pistigorsky. He and his piano accompaniest were rehearsing for a concert to be given in the Château Laurier that evening. When Mrs. Margosches located her daughter and discovered what had occured, she said, "Ask them to have tea with us in Peacock Alley." The two men accepted the invitation.

When Maestro Pistigorsky left, he kissed Sylvia and asked for her address. On his return to New York, he sent the star-struck young girl an autographed photo of himself with his cello in hand.

In 1930 Sylvia was a débutante. She was presented to Governor General, Viscount Willingdon, at the Château Laurier. About that time she often had tea in Peacock Alley and listened to the music of the Armand Weisbord trio. Mr. Weisbord and his group also performed in the Main Dining Room for many years.

Sylvia Margosches was married December 29, 1942 to Arnold Haltrecht. Both their wedding ceremony and the reception were held in the Château. That evening the young couple enjoyed the company of their friends and families, as they danced in the Canadian Grill. Today, Sylvia Haltrecht is one of the volunteer guides who take visitors on escorted historical tours of the Château Laurier. [6]

Armond Weisbord, violin; Wilfred Charret, piano and Helen Longdon, cello.

At the Château

Château staff who worked in the Main Dining Room, the Canadian Grill and in Room Service during the thirties have many memories. Steve Phillips said:

> "My father emigrated from Syria to Winnipeg where he worked at the Fort Garry Hotel. He was a waiter and very good at his job. Later he was transferred to Ottawa to work in the Main Dining Room at the Château Laurier. During my summer holidays in 1935 and 1936, I also worked at the hotel as a bus boy. I worked very long hours, from six a.m. to noon, then went back at 6 p.m. and worked at least until nine p.m. for fifteen dollars a month. When I became employed full-time, I was on duty until midnight or even one a.m. on nights when a banquet was being held, then I had to be back in the Main Dining Room at six a.m. My pay then was thirty-three dollars a month. None of us ever had Christmas Day or New Year's Day off duty.
>
> I remember an incident in the Main Dining Room when a mouse ran across the floor while the room was full of diners. Mr. Poncet, the Head Waiter, was very calm. He succeeded in getting a few screaming ladies down off their chairs.
>
> The March Brothers, designers of Canada's National War Memorial to the dead of the First World War, were guests in the hotel and dined in the Main Dining Room for several months while they supervised the installation of the Memorial. Both it and the Plaza surrounding it were ready just in time for the visit of King George VI and Queen Elizabeth in May of 1939."[7]

Emile Labranche trained as a pantry-man in the Canadian Grill in 1938.

> "My job was to remove all the salt and pepper shakers from the tables and put them back onto their proper storage shelves. Then I took the soiled table linen to be counted before it went to the laundry. I picked up fresh linen and delivered it to the Grill Room.
>
> My Dad, who also worked at the Château, introduced me to the Head Waiter, Mr. Siegrist, and said, 'If he doesn't behave himself, send him home.'
>
> Mr. Siegrist ensured that our appearance was always just right. I shaved at 11:15 one morning and went on duty at noon. Siegrist looked at me and said, 'You need a shave.' Off I had to go to the locker-room to shave again.
>
> The Grill Room closed after lunch at two-thirty p.m. One of my brothers worked there also. After the door was locked one day, just for a laugh I seated him at a table and served him lunch as though he were my

No visit to the Château was ever complete without lunch in the famous Canadian Grill, as shown in this 1939 photo.

favourite guest. No one caught us and of course we didn't tell anyone what we had done. During World War II that brother was killed in action overseas. I'm very glad to have that wonderful memory of him.

I went overseas myself in 1941 with the navy. When I returned I took another job. However, I did work part-time at the Château for the next ten years serving at banquets and other special occasions." [8]

Robert Goyette recalled.

"Charlie Foster, Andy Hammond and several other waiters worked very hard with me in the Main Dining Room in 1938 and 1939. The Captain of our group was Mr. Eugene Poncet. Mr. Helders was Head Waiter. He trained us and drilled it into us that we should always serve from the right and remove dishes from the left. We served breakfast, lunch and dinner in the Main Dining Room, and afternoon tea in Peacock Alley. If we served all four meals, which meant from 6 a.m. to 9 p.m., we were supposed to be paid thirty-five dollars a month. If we served lunch and dinner, we were paid two-thirds of that, and if we only worked one meal, we received one-third of our salary.

Maurice Chevalier stayed at the Château for a week once. He was most friendly and appreciative of the service we waiters gave him.

There were four different breakfasts in the Main Dining Room in the late thirties, ranging from juice, cereal, toast with jam, honey or marmalade and tea or coffee for fifty cents, to a deluxe breakfast of juice, cereal, two eggs, ham, bacon or sausages or Winnipeg gold-eye, toast, tea or coffee at eighty-five cents. If you were really hungry, all of the deluxe breakfast plus sweet rolls or croissants or assorted muffins would stave off hunger pangs for the sum of one dollar.

A favourite dinner of guests in the Main Dining Room was lobster and scallops in a chafing dish, served in a hot seasoned sauce. Another was filet mignon. The whole filet was garnished with every vegetable you could think of, then taken to the table piping hot. There was enough food for six people, and it cost eight dollars." [9]

The price of meals in the Canadian Grill was comparable to those in the Main Dining Room, with dancing included. You could dine and dance there on New Year's Eve in 1934 for five dollars.

A dance held annually in the Ballroom, called Le Bal des Petits Souliers, was given by a group who supplied shoes for underprivileged children of Ottawa and district.

One such occasion was particularly remembered by Goyette.

"One young lady wore a red taffeta strapless gown. She was dancing with her partner when suddenly the dress fell down. The lady was naked. Unperturbed, she reached down, hauled up the dress, adjusted it over her bosom and went on dancing with her beet-faced, embarrassed partner, without a second glance at anyone.

I knocked on a door one morning at breakfast time and was invited to come in by a female voice. When I pushed the door open, the lady was standing on her bed with her nightgown off. It was draped over one shoulder. Other Room Service waiters say it was amazing what went on in some rooms, even when staff were in the room."

In 1940, Robert Goyette went overseas with the Canadian Army. He returned safely and resumed work at the Château in Room Service until 1957.

A staff of fifty young women worked as housemaids in two shifts. They were supervised in the thirties by Miss Jean Stewart, the Housekeeper, and several assistant housekeepers. Miss Jeanne d'Arc Manthe was one young lady who worked on the day shift. Miss Irene Quevillon, on the evening shift, was responsible for turning down the beds ready for tired guests. These maids often found articles left behind by patrons. They turned them over to Miss Stewart, who received thousands of articles this way every year. She kept them in a locked cupboard until she got an S.O.S. from someone to send along the forgotten item.

Mrs. Florence Redmond, an Englishwoman, was Executive Housekeeper when Mr. Aylett was at the Château. By then the number of housemaids had risen to eighty-three. Mrs. Redmond was quite strict with the young women in her department. She also kept her eyes and ears open in all areas of the hotel for any infraction of regulations.

Shortly after arriving at the Château, Mrs. Redmond was asked by a guest to provide a baby-sitter. She was not familiar with that term and she sent a child's commode to the room. Another time when a guest complained of a bad odour in his room, Mrs. Redmond searched the room, but could not find the source of the smell. Finally she noticed a string tied to the radiator and then leading outside the window. When she hauled in the string, two very dead and decaying ducks were hanging from it, forgotten by some hunter.

Mrs. Doris Moulds worked in the housekeeping department from 1932 until about 1940. She worked her way up from looking after linens to becoming an assistant housekeeper. Her most vivid memory was of a day when she opened a window in a guest's room which faced into the centre of the building. She was wearing a lovely old family heirloom watch, sent to her by an uncle in England. As she pushed on the window, the watch-band caught on the window-pull and the watch went tumbling down onto a flat roof several floors below. It was recovered, but was too badly damaged to repair. [10]

Albert Cuthbert was Mr. Aylett's Bell Captain. He controlled fifty bellmen, doormen, lobby boys and elevator operators. He was at the Château for many years and was addressed by his first name by many celebrities. Albert, usually around from early morning until late at night, met every train that arrived during his shift.

Mackenzie Porter recorded a number of stories about the staff in his article.

"Mr. Aylett could depend on his staff to carry on their duties in an extremely capable manner. When he was off duty, he had no worries about their abilities in case of an emergency. When one woman, with the aid of a chambermaid, was packing to leave the hotel, a gust of wind from the open window picked up a flimsy undergarment from a nearby chair and carried it out into Major's Hill Park. 'Oh,' exclaimed the woman, 'I can't leave without those!' The maid phoned the Housekeeper, who called the

Bell Captain. He summoned two of his nimble lads who raced across the park to the tree. As one man hunched over, the other climbed on his back, reached up, grabbed the undies and the lady made her train on time. Mr. Aylett didn't hear about it, he simply expected such service as the norm.

Aurele Seguin, a meat chef and brother of Henri, the bellman, once played a game of chess against a cafeteria customer, Lt. Col. Norman Samuel, without once interrupting cafeteria service. Samuel handed the chess board to Joe Kingsley at the meat counter, and he turned it over to Seguin who made his move during the evening, then gave the board to Kingsley the next day to give to Samuel. The game went on for months.

Joe Kingsley served excellent meals at very reasonable rates in the cafeteria. He was also an institution at the Château who could get away with teasing many of his regular customers. He saw the Hon. Paul Martin wearily pushing his tray towards the meat section in the cafeteria one evening, after the Health Minister had been given a rough time in the House of Commons by George Drew, Leader of the Opposition. 'Well, Mr. Martin,' said Kingsley, 'How about sinking your teeth into one of our lamb chops a là George Drew?'

Another top aide of Mr. Aylett's was Henri Freitag, the Swiss chef who dearly loved it when visitors to the Château requested Canadian specialties such as buffalo meat, bear steaks, saddle of beaver, seal flippers, Winnipeg gold-eye or domestic pheasants. If those items were available, Freitag would go to no end of trouble to acquire them and prepare them. He felt it added to the hotel's reputation.

In Room Service, Mrs. Mabel Egan was in charge. She was said to have a fabulous memory for voices. Once she had spoken on the phone to a guest, she would always remember that voice and be able to put a name to it. One regular guest moved to Japan on business and was away for ten years. When he returned and called Room Service, Mrs. Egan called him by name, saying, 'Your usual order, sir?' Another time, Sen. Ian Mackenzie spent a night at the new Hotel Vancouver. When he called Room Service and gave his order a voice replied, 'Right away, Senator Mackenzie.' 'Is that you, Mrs. Egan?' he asked incredulously. 'Yes,' she said, 'I've been sent out here for a few weeks to help out." [11]

Every Christmas the hotel hosted a party for the staff. A huge turkey was presented to the family with the largest number of children. "It was usually a toss-up between my family," said Emile Labranche, "and the family of Paul Emile (Red) Tassé, the Château Laurier head barber. One year, Dad could see that Red had brought more children than he had, so he rushed home and came back with the three little ones in our family and we won the turkey."

A young man named Roland Boisvenu looked after supplies at the Château, all the while dreaming of becoming a ballet dancer. His dream came true when he won $35,000 in an Irish Sweepstake. He took himself off to New York to study ballet. Roland's father, Hector, was a Bellman for many years.

George Gilmour studied mechanical and architectural drafting at Ottawa Technical School. He intended to work in the field, but in 1936 he took a temporary job on the front door at the Château. He remained at the hotel throughout his working career, except for time-out during World War II when he served overseas with the military police.

When interviewed by Duncan Dunbar, George remembered an Englishman who used to come to the Château before the war.

> "He was a pleasant fellow who left and I didn't see him again. Then the first day I was in London, I was standing waiting to get into a telephone booth at Waterloo Station. I was getting impatient, because the person inside was doing an awful lot of talking. But finally he came out and who do you think it was? That same Englishman! 'Where did you come from?' he roared, and we had a fine time talking over old times at the Château." [12]

Well over six feet tall, with a ready smile for hotel patrons, George Gilmour was a friendly man, an excellent ambassador for the hotel. After the war when he became President of the Château Laurier Union Division 270, the division undertook to form a credit union for the hotel employees. Management was as pleased as the employees with this first in the C.N. hotel system. A small office was provided in the hotel basement where the credit union's operations were carried on after working hours. Later, George Gilmour was promoted to Assistant Night Manager at the Château.

George Holt, Jim (Red) Higgins and Larry Beachill were other well-known Château doormen who gave patrons a very favourable first impression of the hotel on their arrival.

In February 1939, Mr. Van Wyck brought a new Maître d'hotel to the Château from Europe. He was Victor Herbert, an Englishman, who had grown up in Austria. The current Maître d', Mr. Helders was to be transferred to the new Hotel Vancouver due to open in May of that year.

Herbert brought a wealth of experience to the Château. He had worked at the Berkley Hotel in London, England, the Savoy in Brussels, the Winter Palace in Luxor and the Four Seasons in Munich, the latter being one of the world's most glittering hotels. When war seemed most likely, Herbert was eager to get his wife out of Austria. Initially they went to London where he worked in an exceptional seafood restaurant in St. James Street.

With his application for the Château position, Herbert had sent a photo of himself. He appeared tall and distinguished looking and beautifully dressed in white tie and tails. Van Wyck called Miss Lancaster into his office and said, "How would you like to have this man as your boss?" They both agreed he was just what the Château needed.[13]

Robert Pitt met Herbert at the dock in Halifax in February. The poor man was not dressed warmly enough for a Canadian winter. The first thing he had to do when he reached Ottawa was to buy some warmer clothing. Mrs. Herbert followed her husband to Canada a few months later, after the birth of their child. Victor Herbert, a very shy but extremely capable man, proved to be one of the most outstanding employees the Château has ever had.

A Royal Visit

A big boost to the morale of Canadians in 1939 was the expected cross-Canada visit of their Majesties, King George VI and Queen Elizabeth. Preparations went on for weeks at the Château Laurier.

In early May, Van Wyck and Helders rushed out to Vancouver to supervise the opening of the new Hotel Vancouver, a Canadian Pacific Hotel operated by C.N. Hotels as part of a joint venture. One of its first functions was to be a luncheon in honour of the King and Queen.

Prime Minister Mackenzie King had a great deal to do with the preparations for the Royal visit. One thing he did was to appoint his friend and confidante, Tassé, the Château head barber, as 'Barber to the King'. Red would travel across Canada with the Royals and would cut His Majesty's hair and shave him as well. It was thought to be a great honour. Tassé's whole life history was written up page after page, in both official languages, in the Toronto, Montreal, Ottawa and Hull newspapers. As a result, so many rubber-necks arrived at the Château in the weeks before the tour to be shaved by Tassé, that his regular customers had a difficult time getting into his shop.

"It will be a regular barber shop, with the proper kind of chairs, mirrors, basins and all the necessities," Red told Allen Noblston of the *Toronto Evening Telegram*. The shop was supposed to be on the pilot train with the newsmen, but that was changed to the Royal train.

"I'll be looking after all the men on both trains," Tassé continued. "There will be plenty of them. His Majesty, perhaps, may want to be shaved in his own room and maybe I'll do Mackenzie King and some of the others that way. The others will come to the chair by appointment. I'll fix times for them.

I've got it all figured out. I'll do the King when the train is standing still. But the others," he grinned, "they've got to take a chance. If I cut the throat of a newspaper man, there's always two or three to take his place." Noblston continued in his story, "This as he stropped the razor to shave me." [14]

As it turned out, His Majesty brought his own barber with him from England, but Tassé did accompany him from Quebec City to Vancouver and return. He trimmed the Monarch's hair several times on the journey and barbered all the other men accompanying the Royal guests.[15]

May 19 was the big day for the arrival of the King and Queen in Ottawa for their four-day visit. As in other Canadian cities, the citizens of Ottawa came out to see the Royal couple by the thousands. Flags, bunting and pictures of Their Majesties were everywhere.

When Queen Elizabeth entered the Château Laurier Drawing Room where a reception was held in their honour, she was heard to exclaim, "How lovely!". She quickly walked over to the window and looked out at the huge crowd below. "Is there anywhere we could step outside and let them see us?" she asked. Arrangements had not been made for an outdoor appearance at the Château, but Mr. Herbert heard the Queen's request and mentioned it to Mr. Aylett. The two of them got together a crew of carpenters, who worked all night to erect a strong platform with a railing round it, above the front entrance to the hotel. They draped it with flags.[16]

The next evening, when the Royal couple arrived at the Château from Government House to attend a State dinner hosted by the Prime Minister, the Rt. Hon. W.L. Mackenzie King, Mr. Aylett led them to the platform, below which it seemed all of Ottawa stood in expectation. Their Majesties were pleased to be able to see everyone and to be seen. Ottawans were thrilled to see their Monarch and his Queen. She was radiant in a white brocade gown, over which she wore the wide blue sash and decoration of the Order of the Garter. A white fox-fur cape covered her shoulders, and a brilliant diamond tiara was set on her dark hair. The shouts of greeting from the crowd were thunderous.

The State dinner was held in the Ballroom. All the tables were decorated with lighted tapers and boquets of lily-of-the valley, Queen Elizabeth's favourite flower. Members of the House of Commons, the Senate, the Cabinet Ministers and Diplomats were all present.

Steve Phillips, one of the staff that evening, recalled:

"I was waiting on the head table that night and I saw the Queen slip off her shoes and rub her feet together as people often do. She saw that I noticed and she gave me one of the nicest smiles I've ever seen."

The next day, King George VI unveiled the inspiring War Memorial dedicated to the Canadian men and women of Canada who lost their lives serving their King and country in the Great War of 1914-1918.

Not for another six years would there be such a carefree celebration in Ottawa or in any other capital in the western world. Already the flames of war were lit in Europe, ready to be thrown and burst into the greatest conflagration the world has ever known.

Waiter Captain Gadmaire briefing staff prior to a major banquet.

CHANGING TIMES

On May 7, 1945,

the war in Europe ended.

As soon as the news spread

Ottawans converged

on Confederation

Square.

THE CHÂTEAU'S ROLE IN WARTIME

ON SEPTEMBER 3, 1939 Prime Minister Mackenzie King's broadcast announced that Canada would join Britain in declaring war on Nazi Germany. The formal Canadian declaration of war against the German Reich was made on September 10. Immediately, Ottawa burst out of the depression. People poured into the Capital from all over Canada. With housing at a premium, families who had spare bedrooms were asked to take in a war-worker. An Emergency Shelter Administration was set up by the Wartime Prices and Trade Board.

Many of the people in top positions in industry and in government lived in the Château Laurier during World War II. All were responsible for paying their own hotel accounts. But whenever they were out of town, their rooms would be rented out and their accounts adjusted accordingly.

Marcel Provencher, who began working at the Château Laurier as a bell-boy in 1929, had risen to the position of room clerk by 1939. He recalled:

"At that time there were so many requests for rooms that we overbooked by ten per cent and, instead of booking rooms, we booked beds. When the daily trains arrived from Montreal and points east, followed shortly by trains from Toronto and points west, we would stall a bit, take guests' names and say we were arranging their accommodation. Then we would pair up Montreal guests and pair up Toronto guests. They would all end up with a bed but not a separate room. Then we would call everyone and say, 'The best we have is a twin bedroom and another man from Montreal (or Toronto) will have to share with you.' If we had two lawyers or two men from a similar business we paired them up. Most men understood we were doing our best." [1]

Among the many men seen almost daily in the Château halls, either coming or going from meetings or rushing down to the Cafeteria or Grill Room for lunch and a business talk with their co-workers, were nearly all the Cabinet Ministers and their deputies and assistants.

Donald Gordon would appear at the door of the Canadian Grill Room at noon where there was a long line-up each day. He would crash his way through the crowd and go to his usual table without being escorted by the head waiter. "He was a smart man," said Dan Lupino, "but rough and tough."

In 1946, Robert McKeown, a Montreal reporter, revealed aspects of the Château's war-time role:

> "During the war, the Château Laurier was the scene of many a secret conference. Military and industrial leaders quietly entered the hotel by the tunnel from Ottawa's Union Station and went to work. Production and armament plans were laid behind closed and locked doors, while fellow guests passed by unaware down the thick-carpeted corridors." [2]

Travel Difficulties

The combined Trans Canada Airlines (T.C.A.) and C.N.R. ticket office in the Château took on new importance at the outbreak of war. It soon became clear that T.C.A. could not stick to its policy of a 'men-only' staff. Dorothy Pearson Baldwin and Jane Irwin joined Mr. Gordon Wood in the office in October 1940. "We had to learn the ropes very quickly," said Mrs. Baldwin. [3]

Soon the small staffs of both offices were snowed under by the huge volume of traffic. By July of 1943, there was a staff of about thirty people, mostly women, who worked shifts 'round the clock'. They were considered to be essential workers, had their fingerprints taken and swore allegiance to the Crown. Irene Baxter, office manager, trained personnel to exercise great tact and good humour with passengers. The District Manager at that time was W.R. (Reg) Campbell.

The physical layout of the hotel lobby made it impossible for the office to function easily. Consequently, things were rather cramped. One area held two rows of desks where eight young female Reservations Agents were on duty on the daytime shifts, while four covered the evening shifts and one lonely young woman carried the all-night shift.

A direct Red Line taxi service transported T.C.A. passengers to the Ottawa airport. Each departure was announced throughout the lobby and main floor public rooms by a page boy. Sometimes it was difficult to find passengers who had indicated they wished transport to the airport. If they did not answer a second call, the cab left without them. If they showed up later, there was a mad scramble to find another taxi to rush them to the airport.

A system of priorities had to be set up for travel in wartime. As T.C.A. used Douglas DC3 planes which only carried twenty-one passengers, it often became necessary to deplane passengers concerned in non-essential business. That was not a pleasant task for the employees, especially if a passenger who was trying to get to a point at some distance for the funeral of a loved one had to be removed. Occasionally someone tried to throw his weight around by demanding a priority to which he was not entitled. In order to overcome that type of situation, government travellers were issued a priority passenger form duly signed by an authorized person in each department.

Bell Captain's desk in inner lobby.

One of Canada's largest contributions to the war effort was the training of Commonwealth aircrew in Canada. Lord Riverdale, a Sheffield industrialist, headed up the large British delegation which stayed at the Château in October 1939. Negotiations with Canadian government officials led to the Commonwealth Air Training Plan being set in place that December.

A New General Manager

During the winter of 1942, Joseph Van Wyck went to Vancouver on holiday. He had been very ill and hoped to recuperate in the milder climate on the west coast. Sadly, his health deteriorated and he died on March 2. This greatest of Château general managers to that date was mourned and missed by many across the whole C.N. Hotel chain.

Mr. Robert Sommerville, the new General Manager, moved with his wife into a suite on the fourth floor of the Château. "Bob Sommerville was a blond Scot with just a whisper of a burr in his voice," Austin Cross, *Citizen* staff reporter, tells us. "The man who left East Calder in Scotland to become a lawyer, who did bit parts in Hollywood for a season and who ended up running one of Canada's greatest hotel systems, did not get to the top by accident." [4]

There was more to the hotel business than love of people, Mr. Sommerville acknowledged. He stated emphatically that, "the back of the house was just as important as the front. A general manager needed a cash register for a mind in order to show a profit." He kept a little black book in which he recorded when the hotel was in the red and when the figures were in the black. [5]

As happens to most people of prominence, every little idiosyncratic behaviour is noticed. So it was with the new manager. Mr. Sommerville maintained an old hotel manager's adage, which guaranteed success in business if a man changed his suit three times a day. Mrs. Sommerville had a small dog which she used to take into the Jasper Lounge, in the late forties, after the Jasper Tea Room became a cocktail lounge. It was against the Liquor Control Board of Ontario regulations to have a dog in the lounge, but staff hesitated to ask the General Manager's wife to remove the animal.

Doug Small, Ottawa Bureau Chief of Global Television, whose parents were friends of the Sommerville's, recalled:

"I remember having Sunday dinner in the Canadian Grill with Mr. and Mrs. Sommerville. I remember the service we got that night, and the stories he told of a rich and elegant lifestyle, of a life spent almost entirely within hotels, being waited on from dawn to dawn, of summer trips to Jasper Park Lodge, Alberta and private railway cars full of dandies whom he used to take down south to watch the Kentucky Derby." [6]

Hollywood Visitors

An American movie, 'Captains of the Clouds', starring James Cagney and Dennis Morgan, was filmed at Uplands Airport in Ottawa during the war years. Both Cagney and Morgan stayed at the Château where some scenes were shot. Jimmy Cagney wanted to get out in the fresh air one day without being mobbed by fans around the hotel. He asked Chief Engineer Jack Ballard if there was a rear door where he could slip into the park. Ballard let him through a door leading directly onto Major's Hill Park, where Cagney enjoyed a quiet smoke all by himself. Later he presented Ballard with a lighter.

The movie actress, Maureen O'Sullivan, whose husband, Commander Farrow, was a Canadian naval officer, lived in Ottawa during part of the war. Len Hopkins' Canadian Grill orchestra played for the Farrows at a garden party at their home. Actress Mia Farrow is their daughter.

Jack Benny and Mary Livingstone visited Ottawa and the Château in the forties to promote the sale of war bonds. Shirley Temple, accompanied by her parents, came to the Capital in 1944 for the same purpose. Prime Minister King was fascinated by the young actress. He met Shirley and her parents on Parliament Hill, where she spoke in aid of the Victory Loan Campaign. When the official party left the Hill to drive to the Château, the car was surrounded by a crowd trying to catch a glimpse of the child star. King was worried someone would be hurt, as the crowd was so dense it was almost impossible to move. When they finally reached the Château he gave a sigh of relief, but that emotion was soon stifled for they entered the hotel to find the public had been allowed into the lobby. The crush, worse than it had been outside, had only one policeman to control the situation. The Prime Minister managed to hold onto Shirley and get her to an elevator, but they were separated from her parents who made their way to an elevator as best they could. They invited Mr. King into their suite for a chat before attending a luncheon in the Tudor Room given by Mr. J.L. Ilsley, the Minister of Finance. It was a lot of excitement for the ageing Prime Minister. He said in his diary that, in the crush of children around them in the lobby, '... his heart beat very fast and he had difficulty getting his breath'. [7]

The famous Hollywood duo, Jack Benny and wife Mary Livingstone, posed with Prime Minister Mackenzie King (centre) during a 1940's Ottawa visit to promote the sale of War Bonds.

A leading British economist, Lord John Melville Keynes from Cambridge University, visited Canada several times in 1944. He met with the Minister of Finance, J.L. Ilsley, and senior officials of his department and of the Bank of Canada, to discuss very important financial matters between Britain and Canada. In July he had been to the Bretton Woods Conference in New Hampshire to work with committees on the International Monetary Fund and the operation of the International Bank for Reconstruction.

Robert Bryce, deputy at that time to Clifford Clark in the Department of Finance, recalled:

> "Lord Keynes gave a dinner in the Quebec Suite at the Château, to which he invited about two dozen men. These included the Hon. J.L. Ilsley, Louis St. Laurent, C.D. Howe, Louis Rasminsky, Graham Ford Towers, Donald Gordon, Clifford Clark and myself plus a few British men. At the dinner he spoke for over an hour on the history of the Bank of England. His listeners were fascinated by this incredibly detailed speech, given to so few men away off in Canada. The dinner was superb, and the wines excellent. The group wondered how Lord Keynes and the hotel chef had managed such a delicious dinner in wartime. However, by mid-July of 1944, meat rationing in Canada had been eased somewhat." [8]

More About Music

Every evening during the war, the Château Grill Room was jammed with young officers from all the service branches as well as representatives of the Free French, Polish, Dutch and Belgian forces who were stationed in Ottawa. With their girlfriends they danced to the music of the Len Hopkins' Orchestra.

One of Canada's most celebrated pop music bandleaders, Mart Kenney and his orchestra, with his wife, soloist Norma Locke, played at the Château for the first time in 1941, for a Protestant Girls' Club dance. "We went back to play for them twice more," Mart Kenney recalled. "They were a fine group with which to work." [9]

Names In the News

Winston Churchill visited Ottawa in 1940, the same year John Buchan, Lord Tweedsmuir, Governor General of Canada, died in office. Churchill addressed a joint session of the House of Commons and the Senate. That was the occasion of his famous remark, 'some chicken, some neck', in reply to a Vichy French officer who forecast that 'in three weeks England (would) have her neck wrung like a chicken'.

A year later Churchill was back in Ottawa. During his stay, Churchill entered the Quebec Suite at the Château accompanied by the R.C.M.P. Bellman Henri Seguin remembered lighting the statesman's cigar. It was the occasion of a dinner in Churchill's honour, given by the Department of External Affairs with five hundred guests in attendance. Later that evening Emile Labranche served a special brandy to Churchill in his room at the Château. In return the great man presented the waiter with a very long cigar.

Madame Chiang Kai-shek spoke in Ottawa in 1943 on behalf of her husband, General Chiang Kai-shek. She addressed a joint session of Parliament to seek aid for China in its fight against Japan. The first lady of China stayed at the Château Laurier during her visit. Austin Cross wrote:

> "I recall the refined tantrums of Madame Chiang and how she sat in state on a platform above the rest of us in the Ballroom. If ever a person posed as an Empress, it was the veil-covered, pock-marked Madame Chiang. Nor am I apt to forget her 'headaches,' which permitted quick and early withdrawal whenever she wished."

Madame Chiang brought her own satin sheets with her, which the Château laundry handled each day of her visit. The dedicated people in that department turned out beautifully laundered clothes in quick order for all guests throughout the hectic war years.

Wartime

Radio became more important than ever to Canada in wartime. News broadcasts eased the demand for newsprint at a time when lumber was desperately needed for more important uses. One of the famous broadcasters from the Château Laurier studios was Lorne Green, 'the voice of doom' as he was dubbed. He read reports from overseas CBC correspondents Matthew Halton, Benoit Lafleur, Marcel Ouimet and Peter Stursberg. The government used the Château station to keep in touch with the people and also to explain the need for so many restrictions in Canada

War time food rationing became part of daily life. With so many people in the hotel at all times in the forties, one would think it must have been very difficult for the chefs to serve so many people while this rationing was in effect. However, the chefs were adaptable and skilled in making the most of what they had on hand and they managed very well.

Marcel Provencher remembered many of the companies such as General Motors who kept accommodation at the Château on weekdays during the war. The Ford Motor Company's representative, Mr. McGinty, was also there. So too were Mr. Phil Garrett for De Havilland Aircraft and Mr. Fred Smye for the A.V. Roe Co. Smye was wartime Director of Aircraft Production, and later became President and General Manager of Avro. Canadair and Canadian Vickers were represented. Bank of Montreal men were frequently at the hotel. Many of these people had standing reservations with T.C.A. from their home towns to Ottawa on Sunday evening, or early Monday morning and back again on Friday afternoon or evening. Some booked six months in advance.

Harry McLean

No story of the Château Laurier would be complete without mention of its most eccentric long-time guest. He was Harry McLean of Merrickville, Ontario, who lived at the hotel from 1945 to 1948. He was President of H.F. McLean Inc., a construction firm, and also President of Grenville Crushed Rock.

Mr. McLean was a self-made millionaire. He would buy rolls of quarters at the bank, then throw the quarters helter-skelter out the window of his room and watch people scramble for the money. On at least one occasion, he was said to have thrown pails of water down onto the people picking up the money on the street below!

Waiter Robert Goyette recalled:

> "Once I was carrying a tray of one dozen oysters across the kitchen to take them upstairs to a guest's room. McLean, who had a habit of going to the kitchen, was there. He gave the tray a kick, scattering its contents. He laughed heartily at my discomfort, then handed me a twenty dollar bill saying, 'Get another tray of oysters for your guest'.
>
> Another time, McLean scattered a lot of change across the kitchen floor and asked Room Service waiter, Steve Phillips, why he would not pick up the money. Phillips replied, 'I'll take the money if you offer it to me, Mr. McLean, but I won't grovel for it'."

Lily Pons was a guest at the Château during the time Harry McLean was there. He heard that her concert tickets were not selling well, so he phoned Marcel Provencher and asked him to get six tickets for the concert and send them to a Margaret Murphy at a certain address. He also asked Provencher to order 100 red roses to be sent to Miss Pons, with a card saying they were from Margaret Murphy. It seems that Margaret Murphy had worked for Harry McLean and then later for Lily Pons. When McLean went to the concert he could see that only about half the seats were sold. He did not want Miss Pons to play to a half-empty house, so he bought the remaining tickets, phoned the R.C.A.F. at Rockcliffe Airport and said, "Send some airman in quickly for a concert. I'll pay for their seats."

Harry McLean and two guests of his went on a rampage one night in McLean's suite. They tore the chandelier off the ceiling, turned a dresser upside down, smashing its mirror, and really made a mess of the rooms. When McLean was reprimanded by the hotel management, he simply shrugged and said, "Put it on my bill." [10]

The War Ends

On May 7, 1945, the war in Europe ended. As soon as the news spread, Ottawans converged on Confederation Square and in front of the Parliament Buildings, the Château and Union Station to celebrate. It was a night to remember.

By early August, rumours of Japanese surrender were rife. Official word was expected. Prime Minister King was advised on Saturday the eleventh that

William Lyon Mackenzie King as photographed by Yousuf Karsh in 1940.

President Truman had called a news conference for Sunday the twelfth. King began to think of what he would say to Canadians from station CBO after Truman spoke.

On Sunday morning, the Prime Minister, accompanied by Mr. Pickersgill, arrived at the Château Laurier studio. Mr. Bushnell and Mr. Wright of the CBC met them and assured the Prime Minister they were ready for the broadcast. King rewrote his talk. Pickersgill brought a stenographer in from his office and had the speech retyped, expecting at any moment to get word to go on the air.

They spent the whole morning in the studio. Around two p.m. the Prime Minister and Pickersgill were feeling tired and hungry. The latter phoned Marcel Provencher, the Château Room Clerk, and asked for a room on the seventh floor where the Prime Minister could rest until broadcast time. They were given one of the travelling salesmen's rooms. Jack Pickersgill next phoned Room Service and asked for a menu for the Prime Minister. Mrs. Egan answered the phone. She thought it was just a prank as she knew no one would put the Prime Minister in a seventh-floor room. She replied, "I'm too busy," and hung up. A quick call by Pickersgill to Mr. Aylett resulted in a good lunch for the two men.[11]

When nothing was happening by late Sunday afternoon, Pickersgill suggested that Mr. King could record his talk, which Charles Wright would air at the correct time. King made the recording and gave instructions that it not be put on air until after Harry Truman had broadcast his statement.

After King went home, he turned on his radio and heard a broadcaster say, "President Truman has announced the acceptance of the surrender terms by Japan." This announcement was repeated twice, then music was played for a few minutes and suddenly King's complete statement was broadcast. The Prime Minister wondered why the station had not waited until after President Truman himself had broadcast. King was embarrassed about the matter and felt the press would be critical of him, and that his enemies would never let him live it down. However, it was the fault of the CBC in Toronto and U.S. broadcasters. But King fussed over the matter for days.[12]

On Monday August 13, Mackenzie King signed an Order-in-Council for a V-J Day holiday to be held August 14, and announced a day of prayer and thanksgiving for the following Sunday, to be held across the nation. As the Prime Minister drove home to Laurier House that evening, young people were out on the streets celebrating. Six years of the worst war in history were over.

Chapter Nine

GETTING BACK TO NORMAL

G RADUALLY, THE POLITICS OF WAR became the politics of peace. War departments were abandoned and their personnel either absorbed into peace time positions or, in the case of the 'dollar a year' men and women, many returned to their companies. Some remained in Ottawa. Prime Minister Lester Pearson remarked in his memoirs, "Fortunately some of these 'temporaries' remained as permanent officials after the war and did their part in strengthening the high and well deserved reputation of the Canadian Civil Service." [1]

After the war, forty to fifty senators lived at the Château and about the same number of Members of Parliament. Château Laurier Hotel rates for the year ending December 31, 1946, make interesting reading. By 1948 the prices for rooms had increased a dollar or two, meals increased by up to fifty-five cents, the cost of a Turkish bath went up by fifty cents and a swim in the Château pool by ten cents.

Many Château employees who returned from overseas went back to work at the hotel. Others did not. Steve Phillips returned, but found he resented the long hours, low pay and few holidays. He went to Mr. Herbert and said, "I'm leaving." "Why?", asked Mr. Herbert. "Because I understand the hotel wishes all their Waiter Captains and Head Waiters to be European trained. If that is so, what chance of advancement do I have?" Mr. Herbert was honest with him and replied, "Yes, you are right. We do wish our senior staff to be trained in Europe." So Phillips left the Château, went into the insurance business and did very well for himself. He spoke of Mr. Herbert as 'a prince of a guy.' [2] Emile Labranche took a job elsewhere but worked part-time at the Château in the

CANADIAN NATIONAL RAILWAYS

HOTEL DEPARTMENT

Rates for Château Laurier for the Year ending December 31st, 1946

AMERICAN PLAN—Includes Room and Meals.   EUROPEAN PLAN—Room only.

CONTINENTAL PLAN—Room and Breakfast.

R. SOMMERVILLE, General Manager.

ACCOMMODATION	DAILY RATES	MEAL RATES
Single, without bath	$ 3.00, 3.50	Main Dining Room
Single, with shower	4.50, 5.00	A la Carte, also:
Single, with tub bath	4.50, 5.00, 6.00	Club Breakfasts… .60, .75, .85, $1.00
Double, without bath		Table d'Hôte Luncheons
(double bed)	5.00	selections from $1.00
Double, without bath		Table d'Hôte Dinners
(twin beds)	6.00	selections from $1.00
Double, with shower		Grill Room
(double bed)	7.00	A la Carte, also:
Double, with tub bath		Table d'Hôte Luncheons
(double bed)	7.00, 8.00	selections from $1.00
Double, with tub bath		Table d'Hôte Dinners
(twin beds)	9.00	selections from $1.00
Parlour, bedroom, and bath	12.00, 15.00	Dinner Dance nightly, except Sunday,
The larger bedrooms are situated		throughout the year.
in the East Wing; each has		Supper Dance nightly, except Sunday,
combination tub and shower bath,		during the winter season.
rates for which are:		Air-conditioned Cafeteria featuring quick
Single	6.00	service of good food at moderate prices.
Double, double bed	8.00	
Double, twin beds	9.00	

SWIMMING POOL, open daily, except Sunday: .50 per hour
(including swimming suits provided by the hotel).

TURKISH BATHS, Open daily, except Sunday: $1.50 per person.

ELECTRO AND HYDRO-THERAPY DEPARTMENT operated in connection withthe hotel.
Open daily, except Sunday. Rates on application.

Banquet Department, where a number of senior waiters were specially trained to work at banquets for such people as Queen Elizabeth, Prince Philip and other special guests.

Employees at the Château in 1944, restless and dissatisfied with their wages, formed the first Canadian hotel employee's union with the Canadian Brotherhood of Railway, Transport and General Workers Union. Two hundred and seventy other hotels followed. Their first contract was signed in March of 1945, with a large increase in salary to $130.00 per month. By 1952, they worked forty-eight hours one week and forty hours the second week to bring them out to a forty-four-hour weekly average. Two or three years later they went to a forty-hour week. George Gilmour became President of their Local 270 in 1947. Robert Goyette was Financial Secretary, and L. (Butch) St. Pierre was a local representative after 1954.

Visitors of the Forties

Several famous visitors came to the Château in 1946. Field Marshall Sir Bernard Montgomery of Alemein was one. On his way, he spent a few days in Halifax, and the Nova Scotian Hotel wired his dietary preference ahead to Ottawa. In particular he enjoyed lamb chops and roast mutton, cheese, and cream soups. All his food to be served very hot. Omelettes were the only egg dishes he would eat.

When Monty arrived in Ottawa, he was met by army friends at Union Station and escorted through the tunnel to the Château. The whole length of the tunnel was lined with cheering soldiers. That afternoon a tea party was held in the Banquet Room for the Field Marshall, a non-drinker. Robert Goyette was asked to serve at the head table. He was told to wear all of his six medals. "Monty noticed my medals, got up, shook hands with me, asked my name and my regiment and where I had served overseas. Then he congratulated me," recalled Goyette. [3]

On one visit, Winston Churchill, accompanied by Sir Anthony Eden, arrived at the Château after an air-conditioned flight to find himself in a very warm suite. In spite of a huge fan already there, the management had to quickly rent three more. Eden was put in a suite at the far end of the corridor, and the only other person allowed to stay on the floor was an elderly English lady from Lancashire who was a permanent guest at the Château. She heard that Churchill was going to make a T.V. broadcast from a suite on that floor and asked the assistant manager if she would be allowed to sit on a sofa in the hall

Britain's Prime Minister Winston Spencer Churchill on one of his
wartime visits to Ottawa.

outside the suite to catch a glimpse of Churchill. She was not well enough to go down to the lobby to see him when he left the hotel. The R.C.M.P. authorized her request and she sat waiting. As soon as Mr. Churchill saw her sitting there, he went right over and had a chat with her. While Churchill was giving his interview, the assistant manager asked the lady if she would like to go back to her room. "Yes," she replied, "but my knees are so weak, I can't walk." Provencher and a burly R.C.M.P. constable escorted her back to her own quarters. [4]

General Dwight D. Eisenhower visited Ottawa and attended both a cocktail party and a dinner at the Château. Austin Cross of the *Ottawa Citizen* stated, "He was as offhand as anyone could be, which had United States officials on tenderhooks." [5] At the dinner, Prime Minister King officially named a mountain in the Rockies 'Mount Eisenhower' in the General's honour.

Cross continued his commentary:

> "Mayor Fiorella La Guardia of New York City took a very fancy suite at the Château, then sent out to the one-arm restaurant across the street, Bowles Lunch, for a sandwich. 'No sandwich, no interview,' was his ultimatum to the press. Finally the sandwich arrived and we got our interview."

Sir Ramaswami Mudaliar, Chairman of the Economic and Social Council of the U.N. Organization of India, was a Château guest in 1946. Robert Bryce remembered, as Deputy Minister of Finance, when he and Mitchell Sharp once had lengthy discussions with a senior Indian official in his Château suite about possible solutions to India's critical food needs. [6]

Stanley Knowles, former M.P. for Winnipeg North Centre for many years and now a keen observer of the Parliamentary scene from a place of honour in the Commons Chamber, recalled a speech he made at the Château in 1946. He was asked to speak to a group of C.C.F. ladies. Mr. Knowles had been ill at the time, but the illness had not been diagnosed and he told the organizer of the event that she might have to speak in his place. His address had only been underway about three minutes when suddenly everything went dark in front of him. Mr. Knowles asked to be excused as he was not feeling well. He was taken to hospital and examined. The problem was not his eyes; the lights had gone dim in the hotel. [7]

Thousands of immigrants arrived in Canada in the post war years. Among them were a number of Italians, several of whom prospered in the hotel business. Mr. Poncet, Head Waiter in the Canadian Grill, had three Captains, each a different nationality. Gabriel was of Greek origin, Rosmaritza, a Romanian and Gray was British. Dress for everyone working in the Grill was very formal. The Captains wore black ties at lunch time and white ties at dinner. Hard work was expected. One Italian waiter put in long hours, saved his money and returned to Italy where he opened his own restaurant in Rome. Another man, Gottlieb Hildebrande, was lured away from the Château by a Texas millionaire who hired him to run an exclusive club.

The Marian Congress

On the occasion of the one hundredth anniversary of the founding of the Ottawa Archdiocese of the Roman Catholic Church, a Marian Congress was held in Ottawa, June 18 to 22, 1947. Its purpose was to pray for world peace and to honour Mary, the Mother of Jesus Christ. Thousands of people attended from all across Canada. Archbishop Alexandre Vachon of Ottawa was host for this gathering. His Eminence, Cardinal James McGuigan, Archbishop of Toronto and Legate of His Holiness, Pope Pius XII, to the Marian Congress, was the guest of honour. Other Cardinals attended from all over the world.

After a liturgical reception at Notre Dame Basilica, a whole caravan of cars drove the distinguished visitors to the Château Laurier for a reception in the Ballroom, where over 2,000 civic dignitaries were waiting. Members of the Federal Cabinet, the Diplomatic Corps, civil servants, provincial and municipal figures, Members of Parliament and the Senate had all been invited by the Archbishop. Many distinguished prelates from other faiths were also present.

Prime Minister, the Rt. Hon. W.L. Mackenzie King, His Excellency, Archbishop Vachon, the Hon. Louis St. Laurent, Minister of External Affairs, His Worship Mayor Stanley Lewis of Ottawa and His Excellency Most Rev. Ildebrando Antonietti, the Apostolic Delegate to Canada, received the guests. In spite of the size of the Château Ballroom, ordinary priests, reporters and photographers had to stand in the aisles. Never before had the Château Laurier seen such an assemblage of religious authorities and accredited representatives of foreign lands. It led one newspaperman to say that, during the week of the Congress, the Capital of Canada became an international city of peace.

On the Saturday evening at 7 p.m., Archbishop Vachon hosted a dinner for the dignitaries of Church and State. The Hon. Paul Martin was a guest at that dinner. He reminisced, "I sat opposite Cardinal Mindszenty of Hungary. At the very moment that we were dining, the Cardinal's Cathedral in Budapest was being burned to the ground by the Communists." [8] The dinner, which began in an atmosphere of great pomp and protocol, ended in a less formal way. Dignitaries exchanged autographs while bishops from around the world, be-medalled military personnel, humble priests and interested laymen all mingled in friendship.

Donald Gordon

Donald Gordon was appointed President and Chairman of the Canadian National Railway Company in October, 1949. This meant a relocation to Montreal for him and his wife, Maisie. Early in December they moved temporarily into the Château Laurier.

Graham Ford Towers, Governor of the Bank of Canada at that time, gave a farewell dinner at the Château for his old friend and colleague. Friends from all Gordon's various jobs in Ottawa were invited as well as some senior officers

The Mackenzie Avenue entrance of the Hotel's East Wing.

of the railway. There was food, drink and speeches and as the toasts concluded, "Gordon," reported Joseph Schull, author of *The Great Scot, A Biography of Donald Gordon*, "wearing his trainman's cap and his engine-driver's scarf, was making the rounds with his silver-plated oilcan, filling glasses with Scotch." [9]

Before the Gordons left Ottawa at the end of December, he spent a merry evening in a Château room with David Mansur, President of Central Mortgage and Housing Corporation, and other friends.

> "As the scotch flowed and songs rose, guests had begun to complain and finally, with much diffidence, the house detective had knocked and looked in. He had been asked by the assistant manager, he said, to request the gentlemen to lower their voices a little.
>
> The new boss of the railway, and incidentally the hotel, had received the injunction mildly and invited the detective in. He had poured a drink for the visitor, encircled him with a great arm and started another song. The embarrassed recruit was not much help to the chorus, but Gordon was understanding. Solicitously inquiring for the assistant manager's name, he went to the telephone and called him, thanking him warmly for his interest in the proceedings overhead. There was one difficulty, however, 'Your friend you sent up is an awfully nice fellow and we all like him very much, but the problem is that what we need is a tenor and he's a baritone'." [10]

Another time Gordon was staying at the suite he kept at the Château when he was appearing for the first time before the Railway Committee of the House of Commons. The strain of the last month's work in a new job and preparations for these meetings had taken a toll on him and he had contracted a very bad attack of athlete's foot. A friend came upon Gordon in the hotel lobby, wearing carpet slippers. He sat through most of the committee hearings with his feet in a pail of antiseptic mixture. His feet were so swollen he couldn't wear his shoes.

Others of Note

"John Bracken, Leader of the Progressive Conservative Party in 1947, was not a good speaker," Charles Lynch of *Southam Press* told this writer.

> "He was making a speech in the Ballroom and stood with his back to the windows, facing a room full of reporters. Mr. Bracken believed he had his audience enthralled. Instead, the press people were all excitedly looking out the windows at a scene across the river. Eddy's mill had caught fire and the reporters were all watching the fire." [11]

Left, Doorman, George Gilmour awaits Ottawa native, Barbara Ann Scott, Canada's Queen On Ice. Right, Barbara Ann's mother sporting an impressive corsage precedes her daughter and Mayor Stanley Burke at a Château reception honouring her daughter.

Barbara Ann Scott returned home to Ottawa on March 7, 1947. She had just won both the European and World Figure Skating Championships. At a reception in her honour at the Château, Mayor Stanley Lewis presented her with a cream-coloured 1947 Buick convertible on behalf of the City of Ottawa. There was a big furor in the city about the car jeopardizing Barbara Ann's amateur status. The following year she won the Olympic figure skating championship. Three months later she turned professional and then accepted the car which had been stored for her. Patrick Watson, now CBC President, remembers dancing with Barbara Ann at a Débutante's Ball at the Château. At the time, Watson was a student at Ottawa's Glebe Collegiate.

Prime Ministers

On June 28, 1948, Prime Minister, the Rt. Hon. W.L. Mackenzie King announced his retirement in the Ballroom of the Château. He had become a tired old man and the resignation was expected. Still the statement sent reporters rushing to telephones.

The Hon. Louis St. Laurent was installed as the new Prime Minister, on November 15, 1948. Mr. and Mrs. St. Laurent often dined in the Canadian Grill, usually on their own or accompanied by their two sons. The Prime Minister was also a frequent swimmer in the Château pool.

Former Prime Minister, the Rt. Hon. R.B. Bennett returned to Ottawa for a visit in the late forties. He had been given a title by the British and was now known as Viscount Bennett. One of the last things he did before returning to England was to walk into the barber shop at the Château just before closing time, when no one else was there but his old friend and confidante, Red Tassé. "May I stay and chat for a while?" Bennett asked. Tassé locked the door and drew the blinds and the two men talked for four hours. When they shook hands to say good-bye, they knew it was their last chat and both men were in tears.[12]

Barber Tassé was as close a friend to Mackenzie King as he was to R.B. Bennett. Suffering from cancer, he retired in 1949, after thirty years at the Château. When Mackenzie King died at Kingsmere on July 22, 1950, Paul Emile Tassé got up from his sick bed to attend his friend's funeral. Five months later he died at age sixty-two.

Chapter Ten

MEMORIES

*I*N THE LATE FORTIES AND IN THE FIFTIES, the May Court Ball continued to be a highlight of the social season at the Château Laurier. For each year a different motif was used. On Friday, February 4, 1955, the theme was 'An Arabian Night'. Robert S. Hyndman, well-known Ottawa artist, prepared sketches for each Ball for three or four years in a row. From the sketches he painted murals sixty feet long by twenty feet high. They were put up at the east end of the Ballroom. "It was all great fun and took about six weeks to prepare," Hyndman stated. "They were in full colour and sometimes included many of the Ottawa members of the May Court Club, their husbands, etc. We also had to build a large wooden framework to hold the panels. It was quite a production." The murals formed a back-drop for the stage on which a cabaret took place.

Robert Hyndman also told the author:

> "Because liquor was hard to obtain, I would screw twelve little hook-eyes into the underside of the big round tables when we were getting ready for the Ball. Then I put a wire with a loop around each of the twelve mickey liquor bottles and hung them all on the hooks. They were hidden by the large white tablecloths. Each table seated twelve people. If anyone moved a table, it sounded like the carillon bells in the Peace Tower. I don't know if the Château ever found out about it." [1]

The Staff Remembers

Celebrities recalled by Marcel Provencher, the Assistant Manager, were legion. As well as all the Kings and Queens, the great names of the World War II and the Cold War, the Château played host to Greer Garson, Anna Nagle, Helen Hayes, Walter Pidgeon, Raymond Massey, Lauren Bacall, and a hundred other actors and actresses.

When movie star Alan Ladd was at the Château with his son, he tried to show the youngster, in their suite, how to turn a cartwheel. As he flipped himself over, he struck a table and broke his wrist. The hotel manager feared he might sue the hotel, but Ladd dispelled that thought when all he requested was to see a doctor to have the bone set.

Actor Franchot Tone was a guest for a few days before he went up the Gâtineau to fish for the summer. The gigantic boxer-wrestler-strongman, Primo Carnero, visited the hotel and ordered huge servings of Italian spaghetti in the Canadian Grill. When Camilien Houde, former Mayor of Montreal, visited Ottawa he often sat in the Château lobby, where he was greeted by more people than Prime Ministers Bennett and King ever were.

One of the well-known Canadian millionaires, E.P. Taylor, businessman, racehorse owner and philanthropist, called the Château to reserve a suite on one occasion when the hotel happened to be completely sold out. Mr. Taylor's father had just died in Ottawa and it was necessary for him to be there. Marcel Provencher knew Mr. Taylor and Donald Gordon were close friends, so he put Mr. Taylor into the suite Gordon kept as President of C.N.R. However, Mr. Gordon was also expected at the Château that day, but only for lunch with a friend. When management told him what they had done, he cancelled his appointment and went to offer his condolences to Taylor.

Dan Lupino liked to talk about some of the wonderful desserts served to all these personalities in the Canadian Grill. He mentioned the Château's home-made ice cream. The coffee variety was especially good. Another kind had crushed walnuts, maple syrup and whipped cream on top. Nesselrode Pudding featured chestnut maronne sauce over the pudding. Biscuit Tortoni was served in a small cup. It was ice cream blended with nut brittle, made on a marble slab in the hotel kitchen, then crushed. Flambé dishes were also popular. Danny recalled one party of seventy guests in the Quebec Suite, who all ordered Crepes Suzette for dessert and wanted to see them made at their own tables. He and Mr. Herbert each made thirty-five crepes

An exceptional guest Lupino recalled, was a Mr. Grammelspecker from Fort Worth, Texas, who always asked Lupino to call him Grammy. He phoned three times a year to say, 'Danny, I'm coming on Saturday night with four people. Put the usual on ice (meaning two bottles of Mumm's champagne).' Danny was pleased that 'Mr. Grammy' sent him Christmas cards for years.

MAY COURT BALL

Once a year winter doldrums

are forgotten in the festivity

and gaiety

of the

May Court Ball.

Artist, Robert Hyndman, creator of May Court Club murals, with Mrs. Lawrence Freiman.

(Opposite Page)
Above, Lawrence Freiman at a 1950's party in the Château.
Below, Governor General Vincent Massey was the special guest at the May Court Ball, February, 1955.

(Top) Herbie Fripp hams it up for his glamorous audience.
(Below) Guys and Dolls 'May Court style'.

Curfew at the Château

In the late forties and fifties, there was still a curfew for visitors to guests' rooms. They were required to leave the hotel by 11 p.m. Two watchmen came on duty at 10 p.m. and one night manager at 11 p.m. It took one man one hour to do a round of the whole hotel, beginning at the top floor. The other sat in the lobby for that hour and watched who came and went. Then they would reverse the procedure. If there were any noisy parties going on, the watchman took note of the room number and gave it to the night manager, who would go up to determine how loud the noise was coming from a party room, and then how to handle the situation.

In addition a very good man was on the elevator at night. He knew by sight, all the street-walkers. If he took any of them up on the elevator, he would make sure of the room number they entered. Then the night manager would go to those rooms and say it was too late for visitors. Upon leaving he would insert a match in the door. Later he would return and know whether the visitor had left or not by looking to see if the match was still in the door.

One man, retired from a very prominent position, had a lady well known to the Château staff, in his room. The manager phoned him and said it was too late for visitors. When nothing happened, the clerk went to the room with a master key. He unlocked the door and opened it slightly. The hotel guest called out, "In the name of the Father, Son and Holy Ghost, she'll be right out". [2]

The Château Staff Strike

The first strike at the Château happened on a day when the Women's Canadian Club, with over 500 members present, was about to sit down to a luncheon. Mayor Charlotte Whitton of Ottawa had come as guest speaker. The chicken pot pie was bubbling, ready for the ladies to take their first bite, when an upset Mr. Herbert, Hotel Maître d', rushed up to Danny Lupino and said, "The permanent staff has gone on strike; what shall we do? Are any of your serving staff permanent, Danny?" "Yes, they are," the head waiter replied. Mr. Herbert went off to tell the convenor of the luncheon what was happening. He told her they had a limited number of part-time staff who were willing to carry on, but service would be very slow. One waiter would have to serve five tables instead of his usual two. The guests understood and did not complain. Everyone had their main course, including apple juice as a beverage. Mayor Whitton was dead set against alcoholic beverages, even a glass of wine, with a meal.

"We did quite well," Lupino stated, "and cleared away the dishes from the main course, then began serving dessert and coffee when Her Worship beckoned me over and said, 'Get them out of here, get them out of here'." "Who do you mean?", Danny asked. "The staff," the Mayor replied. "Many of the guests haven't had their dessert and coffee yet, your Worship." "It doesn't matter. Get them out of here." A large crowd had come as usual to hear Charlotte Whitton speak. "She was anxious to get on with her speech," the head waiter remarked. [3]

That first strike lasted twenty hours. A second strike lasting for ten days, took place in 1951. Both were disputes over pay. Edith Lancaster said, "Mr. Aylett and the staff pitched in and we all made beds and did dishes. Even some of the guests helped. A Mr. Ed. Simard, President of Marine Industries, offered to help with the dishes. He was curious to see how the huge dishwashers worked. His first job as a young man had been as a dishwasher." [4]

In 1951 all the office employees and management stayed in the hotel for the first three days and nights. After that the union obtained an injunction to stop management from doing the work of the union employees. When the strike was over, Mr. Wallace McCutcheon, later Senator McCutcheon, invited some of the staff to his suite for a party. He was very appreciative of what was done during a difficult time.

Royal Visits in the Fifties

Their Royal Highnesses, Princess Elizabeth and Prince Philip, were at the Château for a reception in the fall of 1951. Austin Cross reported in the *Ottawa Citizen*, "The Princess bravely stood in a receiving line, attractively attired in brocaded satin in a coffee colour. Her very personality, her youth, gave the hotel a lift." [5]

Her Majesty, Queen Elizabeth, the Queen Mother, was entertained at a luncheon given in her honour by the Corporation of the City of Ottawa on November 16, 1954. Mayor Charlotte Whitton presided.

How would you like to stand and shake hands with about 1400 guests in the space of one hour and a half? On October 15, 1957, that is what Queen Elizabeth II and Prince Philip, did at a reception in the Château Drawing Room. It was their first visit to Canada since the young Princess had become Queen. The Royals, together with Prime Minister John G. Diefenbaker and Mrs. Diefenbaker, received a seemingly never-ending line of people which stretched throughout the main floor of the hotel. Albert Cuthbert, the Head

Bellman, did not feel up to announcing the 1400 guests, so Bellman Henri Seguin did the job at Mr. Aylett's request. He called out five hundred and seventy-six names. Mr. Diefenbaker was standing near him and thought Henri was announcing too slowly, so he repeated each name in a loud voice, after the bellman.

After the guests were received, they moved into the Ballroom and adjoining Banquet Room. Both rooms were decorated with huge bouquets of gold and bronze chrysanthemums. Smaller bouquets of mums were arranged down the long refreshment tables. Five-inch-high exact replicas of a Crown, given to the Royal family by Queen Victoria, also adorned the tables. They were made by Chef Casagrande of spun sugar and trimmed with silver dragees. The letters, E II R were piped in icing on the petit fours.

A civic reception in honour of their Royal Highnesses, Princess Elizabeth and Prince Philip, was held in the fall of 1951. The distinguished head table included the Prime Minister, The Rt. Hon. Louis St. Laurent and Madame St. Laurent and her worship, Mayor Charlotte Whitton.

Being an MP's Wife at the Château

In an interview with Mrs. Mary Monteith, widow of J. Waldo Monteith, a Member of Parliament and Minister of Health and Welfare in the Diefenbaker Cabinet of 1957, she reminisced on the role of an M.P.'s wife in Ottawa.

"We had young children whom I needed to be with most of the time. However, I had an arrangement with my sister, whereby she would look after our little girls for five days each month so that I could spend that time with my husband in Ottawa. He was affectionately known as Monty by all his friends and by me.

I took the night train to Ottawa from our home in Stratford, Ontario. I walked through the tunnel into the hotel, where all the staff was really friendly. One of the housemaids even washed Monty's socks when I wasn't there. I joined the Women's Canadian Club and served on its board. We had a luncheon in the Ballroom every month with good speakers.

Monty had a large room at the Château during each session. It had a big bay window, with a desk in the bay. There was also a comfortable sofa and several lounging chairs in the room.

On Wednesday evenings the House was not in session, so we went to the Canadian Grill for dinner and dancing with our friends. Ellen Fairclough and her husband, Nora and Roland Michener, Earl Rowe, Jean Casselman and her husband, Wallace and Eva McCutcheon, Davey Fulton and his wife Pat, Donald and Alice Fleming, George and Fiorenza Drew, and George and Mabel Hees were all with us. Agnes Benidickson, another M.P.'s wife, was my closest friend in Ottawa.

When something important was going on in the House, we wives sat in the Gallery and listened intently. We also had a Parliamentary Wives' Club and got to know each other better. There was always a round of diplomatic and government parties to attend if one wished." [6]

Sailors at the Château

Most of the stories we hear about people at the Château concern the rich and famous. Here is a story of a young ordinary seaman, fresh out of basic training at H.M.C.S. Cornwallis in Nova Scotia, who was posted to the Naval Radio Station Gloucester, twenty-five miles south of Ottawa. W.G. Hillaby and his rather impoverished fellow sailors would hardly be expected to choose the Château Laurier as a central point for a thoroughly enjoyable weekend ashore. But they often did in 1951. Hillaby recalled:

"We could rent a bathing suit and swim in the Château pool for a dollar for the whole day. Beer was cool and cheap in the Colonel By Lounge (the

Snake Pit, as the basement beverage room was dubbed). Patriotic patrons often paid for quarts for the 'sailors in the corner.' Meals in the hotel were out of the question, but friendly waiters turned a blind eye to the fresh cheese, salami and bread purchased at the ByWard Market and taken into the Beverage Room. A 'bunk' for the night presented another problem, but if it was a warm night, a trip to Britannia Beach on a 'Toonerville Trolley' streetcar and a night under the stars on a park bench were rather pleasant. In all, we young sailors managed to have a pretty good time on very little money, with much of the entertainment centred around the venerable Château." [7]

W.G. Hillaby, now Commander Hillaby, stated:

"The Château's staff's firm but friendly attitude contributed much to the good times we had. Those were the days when politeness, civility and plain friendliness were common traits of hotel employees. In the fifties the 'old girl' served the somewhat less-than-great with the same flair and concern as that shown to the great."

Pearson's Campaign

Of all the political conventions held in the Château, the one in 1958 ranks among the most memorable.

Jack Cahill, in his book, *John Turner: The Long Run*, wrote:

"The way Canada chooses its leaders has changed. When Walter Gordon called Lester Pearson three days before the January, 1958, Liberal leadership convention and asked who his campaign manager was, Pearson replied, 'I don't have one.' 'Meet the train at 7 a.m.', Gordon said. 'I'll be on it and I'll do the job for you. And bring along your list of delegates.' 'I don't have a list of delegates,' Pearson protested. Gordon suggested he get the list from his headquarters, but Pearson said he didn't have any headquarters either, and when Gordon asked who was raising money for him, he replied, 'No one.' Gordon booked a suite in the Château Laurier as headquarters and wrote a personal cheque for $3,000, and that was the entire cost of the campaign. Nevertheless, Pearson won on the first ballot over Paul Martin." [8]

Senator Keith Davey reminisced about a bit of fun delegates had at that Convention, in the Château.

"Because Lester Pearson wore blue and white polka-dot bow ties at that time, the committee got a tie company to make up a large number of them at a cheap rate. One day a whole gang of his supporters, each wearing a polka-dot tie, did a snake dance around the main floor and up the circular staircase to the mezzanine floor, just as a gag, to remind people that Lester B. Pearson was their candidate." [9]

Things That Go Bump in the Night

Fires have not been much of a problem at the Château Laurier. Russ Bannock, a retired President of De Havilland Aircraft, told the author of a minor fire which occurred one night after he and two friends had gone to bed. They had spent the evening in the De Havilland hospitality suite, which the company often reserved when meeting with prospective customers. Mr. Bannock and one of the men had rooms side by side. The third man, who had imbibed a bit heavily, was across the hall. About 1 a.m. Bannock awakened to the smell of smoke. He opened his door at the same time as the man beside him. The hall was filled with smoke coming from their friend's room. They called the front desk, then on hands and knees crawled across the hall to bang on the door to awaken the third man. There was no answer. Management and the fire department arrived, opened the door to find no one in the room. The room clerk begged the firemen not to turn their hoses on the whole room as only a sofa was smouldering. It was dragged out into the hall and the fire doused. The room's occupant turned up shortly and wondered what all the fuss was about. He had gone out for something to eat. A lighted cigarette was the likely cause of the fire. [10]

Arson was feared once in the seventies after the third fire in two days was discovered. Firemen were called to put out a minor blaze which had been set in a pile of laundry bags in a lower corridor. The day before, one fire had been ignited in a mail box and another in a pile of mattresses. Little damage was reported. [11]

A flue was built into the hotel to carry smoke from the kitchen grill right up to the seventh floor. Normally the smoke dissipated without any problem. One morning a kitchen worker put a large bag of charcoal on the hot grill, still in its paper bag. Of course the bag caught fire and sent the smoke pouring up through the flue, where it spread into the seventh floor. The assistant manager knew about the flue. He called the fire department and then he and his room clerk dashed upstairs to determine if he was right. The smoke was coming from the flue. "Send the firemen to the kitchen," he said to the room clerk. Someone standing nearby heard this and commented, "Damn fool, all the smoke is on the seventh floor and he is sending the firemen to the kitchen." [12]

One bold thief cracked the main safe at the Château in the mid-sixties. He made off with $15,000 in cash and $8,000 in non-negotiable cheques. The safecracker broke through two locked doors without leaving any marks, then drilled the combination lock to open the safe. Manager Myles Craston said, "The office is patrolled regularly by security guards. This thief must have known his way around." [13]

The Château has had its share of people walking off with 'souvenirs' from the hotel. The most amazing were those which were returned under an amnesty, 'that all is forgiven,' issued by the Château management in 1987 just before the seventy-fifth birthday celebrations. A Sevres china urn and matching candlesticks were turned in, as well as a soda-water siphon, numerous china beer steins bearing motifs of the hotel, glassware and a carved mahogany beaver. All these items were later returned to their 'now rightful owners'.

There has only been one murder in the Château. A prominent Toronto lawyer was found dead under suspicious circumstances. His wife, who had called management and said something was wrong with her husband, was taken into custody by the police but was soon released. Later she was again arrested and charged with the murder of her husband. Following a sensational trial, the woman was acquitted. The room number was immediately taken off the door of that room and it was put 'out of order' because of all the publicity at the time. Later, that room and two others were converted into a suite and occupied for a long time by the Quebec Government.

Occasionally, a troubled soul will use a hotel as a means of ending a life. One man, after taking a shower, jumped out of his bedroom window in the nude and was killed. A second man hanged himself. A young woman went into the Château from the street, took the elevator to the seventh floor, got out onto the roof and leaped to her death to Mackenzie Avenue below. People in the Daly building opposite, saw what happened and called the Château to tell management.

Many old buildings, especially castles and châteaux, have ghost stories to tell. The Château does not have a ghost, but at least two incidents of 'things going bump in the night' have occurred as Patrick Watson can attest.

"I do remember vividly two experiences in a room in the Château. I was awakened at one o'clock in the morning by a sound as sharp as a pistol shot and, sitting up in bed, aware that the sound had come from somewhere in the middle of the room. I approached the table placed there, a small table with a reading lamp growing out of it, and found that the heavy

~ 129 ~

glass ashtray with the C.N. logo etched into the bottom of it was cracked neatly in half. It was not a particularly cold night. There was no conceivable explanation for this phenomenon.

The very next night, in the same room at the same time, I was awakened by a loud sound from the bathroom. Going into the bathroom, I found that my soft leather shaving kit containing all my toilet articles, which I had parked very securely behind the taps against the wall where it could not easily be dislodged, was now at the far end of the room, the noise having come from the fact the bag contained a bottle of shaving lotion and a tin of spray shaving cream. Both these events, trivial though they sound, were inexplicable and left me quite shaken. I will never forget them." [14]

COMING
FULL CIRCLE

The Château today carries her

cherished traditions into

the 21st Century

Chapter Eleven

THE SIXTIES
AND SEVENTIES

M USIC FLOURISHED AS A DRAWING CARD for Château patrons. Bill Luxton, now retired from T.V. station CJOH, recalled:

> "In the sixties the Château management initiated an interesting enter-tainment programme for the Canadian Grill. They engaged artists for a two-week run, with two shows a night. Most of them were Americans. Names like Toni Carroll, Alberto Rochi (a favourite with the ladies), Carmen Cavallero and the Four Aces were among them. There was also a smattering of Canadians, including Joan Fairfax, Priscilla Wright and a rising young star from Ottawa, Rich Little."[1]

Len Weekes, the trumpet player in Len Hopkins' Canadian Grill dance band, had taken over leadership of the band when Hopkins left the Château in 1956. Regular patrons were delighted when Weekes continued the same type of slow, dreamy music Hopkins had played.

Most of the men in the band were from the London and St. Thomas, Ontario area. Included were Doug Gall, Norm Bigras, Scotty Kirk, and Pierre Muir, with Clifford Tripp on the piano. Jack Cook, Nils Lund and Bill Newton were drummers and Len Weekes the leader and trumpeter. They wore gold or red jackets on week nights and formal attire complete with tails on Saturday nights.

Floor shows and amateur nights had been brought into the Grill in the fifties by management. Later, entertainers such as vocalists Phyllis Marshall and Jean Steel, and singing groups such as the Deep River Boys were regular headliners.

Len Weekes remembered one Saturday night when the band was broadcasting over radio station CFRA from 10:30 p.m. to midnight:

> "Playing on the air made me nervous and I made a mistake one evening on the last note on the trumpet. I was so mad at myself, I went into the band room and threw the trumpet against the wall. Of course it smashed and I had to go out and buy myself another trumpet." [2]

When Len Weekes retired, he and his band continued to play for many private groups in Ottawa. Len also began doing daily volunteer work at the Ottawa Civil Hospital. He said it brought him joy when patients he met at the hospital told him he had played an Anniversary Waltz or Happy Birthday for them at the Grill.

In the spring of 1961 a young man named Keith Davey, who had just become Executive Director of the Liberal Party of Canada, arrived on the political scene in Ottawa. For the next five years he continued to live with his family in Toronto, but stayed at the Château Laurier on his weekly visits to Ottawa.

Perhaps, more than any other man, Keith (now Senator) Davey may have attended more political meetings, more breakfasts, lunches, dinners and parties in the Château Laurier than any other person. At that time, Walter Gordon was Chairman of the Liberal Party. He and Davey ate lunch in one or the other's rooms at the hotel each day. Lunch wasn't too important to Mr. Gordon, and if Davey didn't speak up quickly when Gordon was ordering lunch, he didn't get any.

Senator Davey reminisced over lunch with this writer while sitting in his favourite alcove in the Canadian Grill.

> "I often took people to the Grill to persuade them to run for office — such as Joe Green, Larry Pennell, Eugene Whalen, John Munro, Peter Newman, Walter Gordon, André Ouellet. It wasn't unusual when you were in office on the Hill and wanted a private meeting with someone, to go to the Grill. When conventions were on, lobbying was endless in all the rooms used in the Château at all times. There were hospitality rooms and private dinners upstairs. When the Senate Committee on the Mass Media tabled its report, we had all the press conferences in one room and, later, a party with thirty or forty people present. We often had that type of dinner." [3]

Author, Joan Rankin, joins Senator Keith Davey at his table in the Canadian Grill. Natural Heritage publisher, Barry L. Penhale, on the right.

Senator Davey continued:

"Another time friends needed some help for a public relations company in Toronto. I gave them an idea which they carried out. They put on a huge breakfast at the Château and invited Woodward and Bernstein, the two men who broke the Watergate story, as guest speakers.

Hundreds of people from various political parties, the bureaucracy and other important people in Ottawa attended.

All during the Pearson period, the Liberals used the Château and had various meetings in different rooms and ate in those rooms. In the Trudeau era we certainly didn't stop using the Château, but we did use other places which had come available, for a change. In earlier years, there was no other place and we were always at the Château."

Modernization in the Château

In the early sixties C.N. Hotels began the first major re-furnishing programme in twenty-five years. By 1962 when it became known that they dared to plan major structural changes to the Canadian Grill, Senators J.J. Kinley, George P. Burchill and A.B. Baird investigated the matter. They requested an explanation from the Minister of Transport, the Hon. Léon Balcer. The dispute even found its way into Hansard. The Senators and many others did not wish to see the Grill turned into a modern, flashy room with bright lights and loud music. Donald Gordon, C.N. President, sided with the Senators. Château manager, Arthur Mann, announced:

> "Yes, there were to be major changes, but no more. The Grill will be redecorated only, with loving care and affection. Everything will be just as it has been, except that we'll freshen things up and perhaps provide long-requested facilities, such as a more convenient powder room." [4]

When Charles Lynch of Southam News Service saw what was done in the Canadian Grill, he exclaimed, "They haven't spoiled it and the music is still as danceable as ever for all but the very young, and they can't afford the Grill anymore anyway." [5]

A highlight of 1962 was the Château's Fiftieth Anniversary Party, held in the Drawing Room in June. That year there were visits from Prime Minister and Mrs. Ikeda of Japan, Prime Minister Constantine Karamanlis of Greece and Prime Minister Ben Gurion of Israel. As well, the hotel was honoured with the presentation of the Duncan Hines Silver Anniversary Award in recognition of twenty-five years of excellent service.

No stranger to the Château, journalist Charles Lynch attended both the 50th and 75th birthday celebrations. He is shown here in 1987 with Peter Howard, Château general manager.

From the perspective of today, the pay settlement of January, 1963, in the new settlement between the Canadian Brotherhood of Railway, Transport and General Workers' Union and the C.N. Hotels, seems ludicrous. Bellhops, porters, clerks, cooks and maintenance workers were awarded a three-cent-an-hour increase retroactive to March, 1962, and a further two-cent raise on the same date in 1963 and 1964. After twenty-five years' service, an employee would receive a four-week holiday and double pay for work on statutory holidays. [6]

When Mr. Mann retired in late 1963, Myles Craston, an Englishman, became the new manager. With him came seventeen years of experience with hotel management in England, France and Switzerland. Prior to coming to the Château, he had been manager of the Ambassador Hotel in Ghana, that country's finest hotel.

The modernization programme continued with Mr. Craston at the helm. Plans included the redecoration and refurbishing of sixty rooms in the east wing. The Ballroom was completely redecorated, the chandeliers redesigned and enlarged, and the gold leaf decoration on the ceilings and walls renewed.

After the office of the General Manager of C.N. Hotels was moved to Montreal, all office space on the mezzanine floor was converted into four new public salons. The new public rooms were the Renaissance, the Palladian, L'Orangerie and Burgundy, names chosen for their style of architecture. Four other convention and meeting rooms on the mezzanine floor were named after Canadian historical figures: Cartier, Macdonald, Champlain and Frobisher. These eight rooms could provide accommodation for seven hundred delegates. More than two thousand people could utilize the Ballroom and five adjacent meeting and dining rooms on the main floor.

Every vestige of the dear old Cafeteria disappeared when its space was transformed into 'L'Auberge,' a two-hundred-seat coffee shop recreated as an eighteenth-century inn in style and atmosphere. Dr. James Kalenda, Chief Designer of C.N. Hotels, planned and executed the design. A circular fireplace finished in rough plaster and heated by infra-red rays, a covered wishing well in one corner, and pine ceiling beams, wooden table tops, old lanterns and buffets created an aura of old-world charm. Costumes worn by waitresses and tray-boys resembled the dress used by early French settlers who originated in Normandy and Brittany.

Ottawa's Mayor Charlotte Whitton officially opened L'Augberge by dipping a ladle into a cauldron of French pea soup which hung in the fireplace. In her usual blunt way she remarked, "This is the first time since taking office that I've been ladling the soup and not been in it." Also that year, Her Worship presented the armorial bearings of the City of Ottawa to the hotel. The shield and crest were installed over the fireplace in L'Auberge.[7]

Another duty of Mayor Whitton's, connected with the changes at the Château, was carried out on the evening of July 17, 1969, when she threw the switch for an elaborate system of floodlights around the hotel. They were to be turned on each evening from dusk until 12:30 a.m. Some people liked the illuminations; others thought they made the Château look like a Disneyland castle.

A new cocktail lounge, the Cock and Lion, succeeded the Jasper Lounge in November, 1965. The name was chosen to signify the Cock as representing the French clientele and the Lion representing the English patrons.

The Cock and Lion's unique starlit ceiling, inlaid with soft lights, depicted in miniature the major stars and constellations of the northern hemisphere. The work, done by Arthur Lenton and Sons, Ltd., of Ottawa, involved the following men: Henry Layer, John Dubé and foreman Guy Raby. The general contractor for all the work on the Lounge was the Louis Donoto firm of Montreal while C.N. staff architect, H.C. Greenside, supervised the work. Deep red furnishings and a colourful floor-to-ceiling stained-glass door added festive touches to the tranquil background of brick, marble and wood. One section of the lounge was furnished as an old English Inn. Light lunches were served at noon hour. [8]

Twelve young women replaced twelve male waiters who were given other jobs in the hotel, much against their will and over the protests of their union. The Canadian Brotherhood of Railway, Transport and General Workers Union sought an injunction against hiring women in place of the men, but the Ontario Supreme Court ruled against the union. The cocktail waitresses in the Cock and Lion wore short red dresses with white, grey and black printed panels in front and matching cuffs on the sleeves. A boater-style straw hat and a bow at the back of their hair completed the outfit. Soon the Cock and Lion became the favourite lounge in Ottawa, often frequented by the press and known to them as the Cock and Bull. Some of the bartenders were Claude Le Page, Rolly Cusson and Butch St. Pierre, all well known to the regular patrons. When the new lounge first opened, Jack McPartlin, who used to play in the old Colonel By Lounge, entertained at the organ every evening except Sunday.

Next came Julio Whiskey, who serenaded people at their tables with his violin. Two other men in his combo played the bass violin and a guitar. The guest artists who came in the seventies and stayed at the Château for their two-week engagements were jazz musicians and blues singers from New York and Los Angeles. Some of these artists returned several times. As was the practise, local talent backed up the headline people from the U.S.A.

While Jack McPartlin was playing one evening, Ottawan Eddie Baxter and a few of his friends from St. Patrick's Parish Church took their parish priest, Monsigneur John O'Neill, to the lounge to celebrate his fortieth anniversary as a priest. McPartlin played all the elderly priest's favourite Irish tunes. It was an evening he long remembered. [9]

More Changes

Because of changing tastes in restaurant style, the beautiful, old formal Main Dining Room was often not used on a day-to-day basis. Some people felt intimidated by its size and formality. Its name was changed to the Adam Room in recognition of its style of architecture and it became a dining room for very large groups at conventions and special events.

As the renovations continued on into 1965, Mr. Craston discovered a treasure trove of some two hundred water colours and etchings in a storeroom on the eighth floor. Deciding they might be useful in the hotel's redecoration programme, he called in Mrs. Denise Grankowska from Montreal, the C.N.'s adviser on art. She discovered the paintings were all by French artists, and some of them, dating back to 1820, were quite valuable. They had been used in the original decoration of the Château when it opened in 1912.

Mrs. Grankowska carefully sorted out the large collection, classifying the pictures according to value and general interest, a task which took many hours. The whole collection was then carefully placed in an empty hotel room. That night the hotel was overcrowded and the disused room in which the art was stored had to be opened up for a guest. The paintings were hastily removed, with no regard to how carefully they had been sorted, and were put elsewhere. "We had to recall Mrs. Grankowska to sort them all over again," said Mr. Craston. "This time we put them in a safer place." [10]

A Potpourri of Happenings

The Rolling Stones group booked into the Château in April 1965 under their individual names rather than the group's name. It was some time before the management realized who these guests really were. By that time boisterous fans were trying, by any means possible, to gain entrance to the hotel. One of the doormen, Gilles Robineau, required four stitches to close a gash over one eye when he was struck by a teenager attempting to get in. A C.N.R. policeman, Constable George Mosuik, was hit in the face and knocked down by a young man who had already been ejected from the hotel.

Two very different occasions in the life of John Diefenbaker took place at the Château. In 1964, at the Conservative Party's annual meeting, he was cheered and received a triumphant response to his speech. It was a night of high drama. Two years later, in 1966, delegates gathered at the Château in an atmosphere of tension and white-hot feelings against Diefenbaker. When he tried to speak he was booed into silence. It was a demonstration against a party leader unique in our history.

Prime Minister the Rt. Hon. John Diefenbaker was honoured by the Kiwanis Club of Ottawa in a Château Laurier ceremony.

Before Pierre Trudeau became Prime Minister of Canada and moved into 24 Sussex Drive, he lived at the Château for three years. Not being one who preferred to tend to daily domestic duties, the service and atmosphere of the Château suited him very well.

1967 Centennial Year

The extensive modernization programme was finally completed just in time for the Centennial Celebrations. These changes resulted in the refurbishing and redecorating of all public rooms, air-conditioning throughout the hotel, colour TV in every room, new convention halls and free parking for an extra 400 cars.

Canada's centennial year was one of the busiest in the Château's history. Between April and October, fifty-four heads of state or their representatives paid good-will visits to Ottawa. Haile Selassie, Emperor of Ethiopia, was the first to arrive. Prince Philip was there in April, for the fiftieth anniversary of the Battle of Vimy Ridge. He returned with Queen Elizabeth for Canada's birthday celebration on July 1. Every day all the special rooms were booked. Often four or five wedding receptions took place in one day during this year of celebrations.

Château Chefs

The executive chef who would oversee the millions of meals for all these guests was Angelo Casagrande. He literally joined the Château staff through the back door at the age of twelve years.

> "Although I was only twelve I wanted to get a job during the Depression to help my family. My older brother who was already working at the Château told me to come down to the hotel and try. So one morning I arrived at the back door to see the chef. He took one look at me and said in a gruff voice, 'Why aren't you at work?' I looked so much like my brother that he had mistaken me for him. I was so frightened I didn't know what to say, so I just went over and put an apron on and started peeling vegetables." [11]

The chef didn't find out about his mistake until the next day, but he decided to keep Angelo on anyway. By 1964, Casagrande had been elected National President of the Canadian Federation of Chefs de Cuisine, a past chairman of the Board of Directors of the Federation, and was known internationally for awards he had received in the field of culinary arts, including silver cups for his ice-carving displays in Canada and the U.S.A. He spoke English, French and Italian, and used all three languages in supervising his large kitchen. In 1971, he completed thirty-eight years of service with C.N. Hotels.

As well as being a renowned chef, Angelo Casagrande was good at finances and knew how to keep the hotel food budget in the black. His brother Tony was also a chef at the Château, a man well liked by all the hotel staff. The two brothers were considered the 'Kings of Chefs' in the Ottawa area for many years.

Another chef of renown at the Château was Godfried (Fred) Beets, who came to Canada in 1948, from Wilerotgen, Switzerland. Joining the Château staff in 1950, Beets was noted for his skill at ice carving, which he acquired in his homeland. The main tools used were wood chisels. He would use three-hundred to four-hundred-pound blocks of ice for statues, flower vases, and other designs. It took him three to four hours to carve a small piece, longer for the larger sculptures. The ice had to be at the right temperature. If it was too cold, stress lines would appear and the ice would crack. If it was too warm, it would have to be re-chilled. All the carving was done in the refrigerated rooms at the Château.

The 1967 May Court Ball

On January 27, 1967, under the patronage of Their Excellencies, Governor General and Mme. Georges Vanier, the May Court Ball was a most elaborate affair. Unfortunately, both the Governor General and Mr. Lawrence Freiman, Chairman of the Ball, were ill and unable to attend. Her Excellency was guest of honour, and Mrs. Freiman acted as co-chairman with Mrs. R.W. Desbarats. All the head table guests were piped into the Drawing Room by Corporal George Brown of the R.C.A.F. Rockcliffe Pipe Band.

Bill Luxton, Master of Ceremonies for the evening, recalled:

> "The dress was formal and I was in rented white tie and tails. The Esquires, a local group, sort of Ottawa's answer to the Beatles, played for the young crowd in the Adam Room. The Bill Jupp orchestra played in the Ballroom and featured the Big Band music of Glenn Miller and Tommy Dorsey." [12]

Henri Seguin remembered wearing an eighteenth-century costume with a powdered wig for the occasion and announcing the guests as they arrived. A towering May Pole, a replica from an earlier era, stood bathed in light and was decorated with Gerbera daisies and fragrant hyacinth bells. At the centre of the May Pole were mannequins dressed in period costumes. Included were a formal gown with a bustle from the time of Confederation, a cycling outfit, a dress from the flapper era and an old-fashioned bathing suit.

Stories From the Sixties

As indicated, the Château was packed in 1967. Gaston Belisle, a long-time Canadian Grill waiter said:

> "Three of four bus loads of people would go to Montreal for the day to see Expo, then return to Ottawa for dinner in the Grill and to enjoy the entertainment here. We were rushing until late at night, then had to be back early in the morning to serve breakfast to hotel guests.
> When Mr. Alexei Kosygin visited from Russia that year, he had dinner in the Grill. One waiter looked after him all evening and when he left, the waiter went outside to watch Kosygin leave by car. An R.C.M.P. constable asked why he was standing there, and when the waiter told him he worked in the Château the constable didn't believe him. He was put in jail for the night. His mother had to bail him out in the morning." [13]

Biaggio Tarddio, another waiter of long standing in the Grill, told the writer of an embarrassing moment for him when he was serving a man from the Russian Embassy.

> "I dropped a pot of mustard on the floor and the guest was so startled that he leapt off his chair and startled me as well."[14]

A third Canadian Grill waiter, Ronald Albert, stated:

> "Diplomats used to come to the Grill in the sixties and bring their children. There was one small girl in a high chair. I would stand behind her father and make funny faces at her and the father never knew why she was laughing so much. I watched that child grow up and always looked forward to her visits.[15]

All three waiters agreed that they enjoyed almost everyone they served. Many people were so pleasant that it gave them the incentive to do something extra in the way of service to them. If they found some to be difficult and were unable to satisfy them, they would call the Maître d'hotel to speak to the individuals and smooth over the situation.

More Official Changes

The year 1968 brought more changes in management. Mr. Craston was named Assistant General Manager of all C.N. Hotels. He was succeeded by W. Gordon Foster, former manager of the Fort Garry Hotel in Winnipeg. Foster was a native of Antigonish, Nova Scotia, who had joined C.N. Hotels in 1930. Two of Mr. Foster's most memorable guests at the Château were Marshall Tito of Yugoslavia and Premier Alexei Kosygin of the U.S.S.R. He thought Mr. Kosygin had a most interesting and impressive manner, and very intelligent eyes. [16]

Myles Craston, assistant general manager CN Hotels, was feted by the staff of the Château Laurier in September 1968, during his last day as manager. Tony Popyk, captain-Canadian Grill, in his 30th year of hotel service, extends congratulations to Mr. Craston while others representing bellmen, housekeeping section, room service, laundry and accounting await their turn in the reception line.

Bellman of the Year — Henri Seguin

A singular honour was paid to Château Laurier Bellman, Henri Seguin on December 7, 1968. At Denver, Colorado, he became the first winner from outside the United States to ever gain the coveted 'Bellman of the Year' Award, in the third annual quest conducted by the American Hotel and Motel Association and the Samsonite Corporation. Seguin was presented with a $500 U.S. Savings Bond, a special four-piece set of Samsonite luggage, a plaque and an all-expenses-paid trip to the convention for himslf and his wife. Henri remarked:

> "I received the award not because I was better than some others, but because I had the opportunity to work for all the V.I.P.'s I served at the Château. I had to make a speech and they made me 'Citizen of the Year.' My wife and I were given a dinner at a lovely restaurant. I wondered why

The 25 year club in 1968 with Mgr. Gordon Foster in foreground.

people were staring at me, but then I noticed a big picture of myself on the wall. Mr. Ed C. Leach, President of the host association said that more than one thousand nominations had been made in the search for the 'Bellman of the Year', and added, 'Henri's accomplishments have made a significant contribution to dramatizing the many opportunities for rewarding careers in the innkeeping industry today'." [17]

Liberal Leadership Convention — 1968

Patrick Watson recalled the evening of the leadership vote:

"I remember vividly the night of Pierre Trudeau's election to the leadership of the Liberal Party, going back up to the Château after the event was over, having been invited to a celebration party in Mr. Trudeau's suite. In the main hall I encountered the late Fernand Cadieux, one of Canada's greatest intellectuals and a close and important adviser to Mr. Trudeau. Cadieux and I had passed many fascinating conversations together in various bars, particularly the late, lamented Cock and Lion, largely talking military strategy; he was a great fan of Clausewitz and a prodigious reader in military and political history.

I said, 'Hello, Fernand, are you going up to the celebration party?' 'I think not,' said Cadieux, looking a little wistful. 'Why?' I asked. He said, 'I can see them gathering like flies around the honey and I think there should be inscribed around the walls of this room we are standing in, in letters of fire, the words, Lord Acton! Lord Acton! Lord Acton!' He was, of course, referring to Lord Acton's famous declaration that 'all power tends to corrupt and absolute power corrupts absolutely'." [18]

A Strike Looms

In October, 1970, the Federal Labour Minister, Bryce Mackasey, said prosecution would proceed against the Château Laurier for not paying its employees the federal minimum wage of $1.65 an hour. The hotel claimed it came under the provincial rate of $1.50 an hour. A threatened strike in 1972 was averted when the staff ratified a new work contract which would give the employees an increase of thirteen per cent in two years, seven percent in the first year and six per cent in the next. Split-shift workers would receive an additional one dollar per day. After eight years employment, workers would be entitled to three weeks vacation. [19]

In 1973 Butch St. Pierre retired from his job as a bar man at the Château, but retained his job as representative for Château employees in Local 270 of the union until 1985. When asked if he felt militant towards management when he was negotiating salaries with them, he said:

> "No. If management was willing to bargain in good faith, I would go half-way to meet them and my word was as good as my bond. I only had one manager who still wanted to keep the 'master-servant' relationship and would not give an inch in negotiations." [20]

Behind the Scenes

In 1972 Miss Violet Stuckey had been at the Château for six years as Executive Housekeeper. She had begun her hotel career as a maid at the Château in 1941, then moved upwards as a housekeeper's clerk and as a relief assistant housekeeper. Later, she was transferred to the Charlottetown Hotel, next to the Prince Arthur Hotel, Thunder Bay and on to the Fort Garry in Winnipeg before returning to the Château. Miss Stuckey recalled the variety of articles people leave behind in hotels. One woman left a mink coat for four days. The most common articles abandoned were false teeth, razors, books, nightgowns, briefcases, pills, shoes and men's rubbers.

The next Executive Housekeeper, Miss Myrtle Tostowaryk, a native of Winnipeg, had held housekeeping positions at the Queen Elizabeth Hotel in Montreal and the Fort Garry in Winnipeg before coming to the Château. She also was amazed at the number of things left at the Château. She even had an S.O.S. from California to send a child's forgotten blanket as quickly as possible, because the child couldn't sleep without it.

Two men whose dedication Miss Tostowaryk appreciated were the Head Houseman and the Public Rooms Houseman. The former always knew where everything was and where to go to find what the housekeeper needed. He was observant in noticing things which needed to be done and in bringing them to her attention. The man responsible for the Public Rooms was responsible for the maintenance and polishing of all brass in his area, the cleaning of all glass doors and the cleanliness of all washrooms and replacement of all the supplies, from cleaning materials to ashtrays.

Because of the Château's proximity to Parliament Hill, Major's Hill Park and the War Memorial, each time there is a public event at any one of these locations, such as the Changing of the Guard, Memorial Services, Canada Day Celebrations or the Festival of Spring, the Château is deluged with people using its washrooms, making extra work. At times like this, the cleaning staff are doubly appreciated.

Near panic must have struck the Room Clerk's department on Tuesday, May 24, 1972, when eighty Grade 6 pupils and their teachers from Don Mills, Ontario arrived at the Château at night, only to find their reservations, made long in advance, were lost. Eighty folding beds were hauled out of storage and set up in the Ballroom and Drawing Room. By 2 a.m., the children were all settled for the rest of the night. On Wednesday, rooms were found for all of them regardless of heavy bookings. [21]

Geoffrey Garside

Mr. Gordon Foster retired as manager of the Château Laurier on September 1, 1972. At a retirement party, Miles Craston, C.N. General Manager, presented Mr. and Mrs. Foster with a miniature bed. The real thing, a queen-size bed, and Mr. Foster's retirement gift, was delivered to their home.

Geoffrey Garside, who at twenty-seven became the youngest manager of the Château Laurier, succeeded Mr. Foster. Mr. Garside, a native of England, had been with the Château for two years and previous to that, had managed a hotel in the West Indies.

The Leader of the Band

In the mid 1970's, the new band leader for the Château was Moxie Whitney, the renowned musician who had played in the Imperial Room of the Royal

The popular Moxie Whitney and his orchestra were great favourites with Grill patrons.

York Hotel for twenty-three years. He was also musical director and talent co-ordinator of all Canadian Pacific Hotels until 1971. He remained at the Château Grill for ten years.

Whitney's big band sound was composed of only five players. Each member, including himself, played several instruments. Among Moxie Whitney's many triumphs was the discovery of a number of 'unknowns' such as Anne Murray and Rich Little. Whitney was the official greeter and master of ceremonies when the band performed. Numerous times he went to a table to introduce himself to guests. He often gave a song's history when it was announced. [22]

For the Children

In 1970, a Christmas tradition began at the Château. Without any explanation, about forty gifts appeared at the foot of the huge Christmas tree that decorated the lobby.

> "No one knew who placed the gifts there or why. The gifts were taken to the children's ward of the Ottawa General Hospital. There were just enough presents to go around, and it made the children who had to be in hospital over Christmas very happy.
>
> Gifts are appearing under the tree again this year, but this time the staff knows where they are coming from. The hotel organized a campaign to collect enough gifts for the children of the Ottawa General Hospital and Sacred Heart Hospital in Hull, Quebec. On December 23, bartender Aldege Whissell, the Château's Santa Claus, and the Hon. Lucien Lamoureux, Speaker of the House of Commons, as well as the Chairman of the Board of Trustees of the Ottawa General Hospital, presented the gifts to the children." [23]

Other features for children began appearing in the Château's roster of entertainment. On Saturday, April 9, 1977, more than six hundred children, aged five to thirteen, participated in the Rotary Club's seventh annual egg-painting contest in the Château Convention Hall. The contest was part of the Rotary Club's Easter Seal Campaign for crippled children. For one dollar an egg, parents could let their children loose to paint the eggs. In the process, a lot of red, yellow, green and blue paint was spattered around the room. The event is so popular that each year there has been a line-up to get in. [24]

(Opposite) Senator Florence Bird, former chaiman of the Royal Commission on the Status of Women. The Hon. Marc Lalonde, Minister responsible for the Status of Women, at her right, October 15, 1975.

Changes for Suite 110

In 1977, the Embassy of Greece moved out of the Château Laurier, as they needed more space. Suite 110, the same suite built as a residence for Prime Minister R.B. Bennett, had been established as a Greek Legation in 1942, and then elevated to Embassy rank in 1945. The suite contained a large drawing room, an elaborately panelled dining room, an oak-beamed study, a spacious kitchen and sumptuous bedroom suites. Most of the furniture belonged to the Château Laurier, but each of the nine envoys' families who occupied that suite over the years added their own personal belongings from their travels and postings in other countries. [25]

After the disastrous fire at the Rideau Club in the fall of 1979, the suite became the new headquarters for the club. There was one member in the club at the time of the fire, the Rt. Hon. Roland Michener, former Governor General of Canada, who got out safely just before the fire burst out on the upper floors. The building on Wellington Street, facing the Parliament Buildings, was a charred ruin.

Once in their new quarters the Rideau Club held its annual black-tie dinner at the end of November. One hundred and thirty guests listened to a speech by His Excellency Governor General Edward Schreyer. The evening helped overcome the memories of that upsetting year.

Chapter Twelve

As Gracious as Ever

N<small>EW HOTELS AND MOTELS</small> were being built in Ottawa in the seventies and early eighties. They began to cut into the business which the Château Laurier had enjoyed for many years, almost as a monopoly. C.N. Hotels realized either they would have to fight back aggressively to regain their place in the market or the Château Laurier would go under.

There was no doubt about it. The hotel had become rather shabby and had lost its place as number one among Ottawa's hostelries. Something had to be done. Early in the 1980's the Château was given its own General Manager, Denis Beaulieu, and an Executive Assistant, Jacques H. Favre. Plans were made for yet another and more drastic renovation, with remodelling and refurbishing to begin in 1983 and to be carried out over a period of three years. The Château would not be the largest hotel in town, but it would become the finest, Mr. Favre declared. Rumours abounded. The Canadian Grill was to close, the Canadian Grill would not close; the hotel would be placed under the management of the Hilton Group, the Château would be saved from the Hilton Group; the Château would be taken over by the government as an annex to the Parliament Buildings (not a serious rumour), and so on.

Despite all the talk it was not until 1983 that work would begin. In the interim, new executives with a great deal of experience in their departments were brought in to keep up the standards the Château had set before. One of these men was Bernie Gillis, who arrived at the Château in 1980 as Assistant Maître d' in the Banquet Department. The next year he was appointed the Assistant Banquet Manager, and in 1982 he became Manager of the Canadian Grill.

Mr. Gillis had a varied career in food services in New York and Ottawa, and from 1973 to 1980 had been Maître d' in the Main Dining Room at the Celtic Lodge in Nova Scotia. In an interview with the author, Gillis recalled several 'Royal' events at the Château. One was a gala dinner in the Ballroom in 1980, in honour of Queen Elizabeth and Prince Philip. Another was when Prince Charles and Princess Diana attended a function at the Château and the lights went out. Everything in the hotel had to be done by candlelight and an un-ruffled Prince Charles made his speech despite the situation. [1]

In 1982 the Ballroom scene from the made-for-TV-movie, 'Little Gloria: Happy At Last', was filmed in the Château Laurier Ballroom. The movie starring Christopher Plummer, Angela Lansbury, Maureen Stapleton, and Bette Davis, featured the life of Gloria Vanderbilt. The whole set was orchestrated by Gerry Arial, floral designer par excellence and owner of the Silver Rose flower shop in the Château Laurier. He co-ordinated all the props including chairs, tables, linens, silver, china, crystal, flowers, and candles. Among the flowers depicting the opulent period were sweet peas, lily of the valley, spirea, European peonies, snapdragons and open pink bridal roses.

Christopher Plummer and Lucie Gutheridge in a scene from 'Little Gloria: Happy at Last'.

Ottawa florist Gerry Arial artistically orchestrated the entire set of the 1982 made-for-TV-movie based upon events in the life of Gloria Vanderbilt.

"The whole film crew came to the Château for seven days and eight nights. They reserved forty rooms and suites. The Ballroom was booked for one week at $1 000.00 a day. The furniture for the scene was rented from a firm in Montreal which specializes in period furniture.

Chef Azema of the Château prepared all the food. The stars simply tasted it at each filming, then it was thrown out and fresh food used the next day. Film was shot morning, noon and night for three days. From all that film only seven minutes of television covering the Château scenes were shown in that movie."[2]

The Château loves celebrating birthdays, especially its own. The seventieth birthday party took place on June 1, 1982, and was open to the public from 11 in the morning. Mayor Marion Dewar arrived for the occasion in a horse-drawn carriage and was greeted at the door by Assistant Manager, Alistair McLean. Champagne, sandwiches and cakes were served. Included was a huge birthday cake which Mayor Dewar cut. The event was made even more exciting by the fact that all the actors and actresses from the film, 'Little Gloria: Happy At Last,' attended the birthday party dressed in the period clothes they wore in the film.

Summit Conference

In 1983, during the Summit Conference involving Prime Minister Margaret Thatcher of Great Britain, Prime Minister Suzuki of Japan, Prime Minister Spadahini of Italy, Chancellor Helmut Schmidt of Germany and Prime Minister Pierre Trudeau, was held in Ottawa before the round of hotel renovations were to begin. All the visitors stayed at the Château. Limousines were to take the delegates from the hotel to the Government Conference Centre located immediately across the street, in the building that was formerly the Union Station, then back again to the hotel. After one session, Chancellor Schmidt decided to walk across the street, which he did, and entered the Château through the front door. Security men were distraught when he disappeared and didn't show up in a limousine waiting at the Mackenzie Avenue door. He was politely requested not to wander off on his own again. [3]

Politics and Press

Mike Duffy, then the CBC correspondent on Parliament Hill, recalled:

> "At the Constitutional Conference in 1982 the various Provincial Premiers had suites at the Château. They were all meeting in Premier Stirling Lyon's room to decide whether they would go along with the Federal Government or tell Trudeau to get lost.
>
> Tensions were very high. There was a mob of reporters and photographers on Premier Lyon's floor and as each Premier got off the elevator, they were beseiged by the press and asked for their comments. When Premier Hatfield of New Brunswick came along, he said "All I can say is that I can get into Studio 54 and into Regine's in New York, but I can't get into some joint in Ottawa called 'Arnold's'."
>
> None of the press knew what Hatfield was talking about. On looking into the incident, it was found that the story was the result of a particular incident. Because of all the tension and pressure from the newsmen, a party had been planned so that the Premiers and Provincial Attorneys-General could relax where no one would know them and bother them. It was held at a disco and restaurant called Arnold's at Rideau and King Edward Streets. When Premier Hatfield arrived the restaurant was full. He did not identify himself and the doorman refused to let him in. [4]

Mike Duffy indicated that he has learned much about politics at the Château. He remembered being present at one meeting of Young Liberals and being fascinated by the way Young Liberals and, in fact, the way all youthful delegates operate. This particular meeting was in the ballroom of the hotel. As the evening wore on, more and more people left, and those who were still in attendance voted unanimously to legalize marijuana. Then they blabbed what they had done to a reporter who was in the hall outside — Mike Duffy.

Changes: Innovations and Casualties

Remodelling and renovations did begin in 1983. For two years the hotel was in a constant uproar. Hammers banged, saws buzzed, dust flew. The Housekeeper and her staff were run off their feet. With the front entrance of the Château and the Mackenzie Avenue door closed off, guests entered the hotel by the door on the west side.

The Executive Assistant Manager, Mr. Jacques Favre, played a major role in the new plans. Like many of his predecessors, he had considerable hotel experience before coming to the Château in 1980. He was a native of Switzerland, and had trained there and in London, England. His working career took him to Zurich, South Africa, Montreal, Toronto, Hong Kong, Switzerland again and finally the Château Laurier in 1980.

In January 1984, Mr. Favre, revealed the changes:

> "The Cock and Lion Lounge will be closed, and in its space shops will be located. Because the roof can be opened at that point, it is planned to put in skylights.
>
> Plans for Peacock Alley are that it will be closed and turned into a restaurant. The space occupied by the Convention Hall on the east side of the main floor will be turned into a new lounge and restaurant called Zoé's in honour of Lady Zoé Laurier, wife of Sir Wilfrid Laurier. The whole front of the restaurant facing Rideau Street will be glassed in. Guests will be able to watch the world go by. The reservations desk will be moved from the inner lobby to the front section on the west side." [5]

The sad part of Mr. Favre's announcement was that the Canadian Grill would close. "It is too big," he stated, "and has been losing money for years. It will only be used as a special occasions room." Ottawans protested the loss of the Grill. In time, this unfortunate decision was to be reversed and the Grill would once more be open to the public.

Another casualty of change was the Château Laurier barber shop. Mr. Beaulieu, General Manager, asked Vincent Boileau to close his barber shop as the space was needed to make room for the accounting department, computers and the telephone switchboard. These operations had to be moved out of the lobby when the renovations were begun. Rick Brennan, *Citizen* staff writer, wrote, "Vincent Boileau held heads of state in the palms of his hands for thirty-three years, but as of next week he'll be out of a job." "I keep hoping that they'll give me another spot in the hotel, but it doesn't look that way," says the sixty-one-year old, who has cut the hair of Kings, the Shah of Iran and prime ministers. Brennan went on, "You can almost see his mind drift back to the good times of the 1950's and early 1960's when there were six barbers going constantly, giving shaves and haircuts. There was even a manicurist and a shoeshine boy."[6]

Boileau recalled:

> "Prime Minister St. Laurent used to come every Saturday between 1948 and 1957, around 10 a.m. In those days he walked in by himself, no bodyguards or anything, and sat down. He would never make an appointment but waited his turn. People would ask him to go ahead of them, but the Prime Minister would always say, 'No'. He was a very friendly man.
>   The only time I was nervous cutting someone's hair was in 1967, when I was called to the Governor General's house to do King Constantine's hair. I guess it was the fact he was a king that made me nervous."

Another Château meeting place which became a casualty was the Cross Keys Pub on the mezzanine floor. Ayala Designs Ltd. of Great Britain had shipped panels, knick-knacks and bric-a-brac by container ship to set up this authentic replica of an English pub in 1973. Whenever this writer took visiting relatives from England to the Cross Keys for a drink, they felt right at home. The pub was replaced by an executive board room.

Celebrations Continue

In 1984 Banquet Manager Pierre Loewenberg noted that despite the work going on in the hotel and all the dust, bookings were still being made for conventions, dinners, cocktail parties and banquets. Three Swedish businessmen visiting Ottawa were heard to declare they would rather stay at the Château Laurier, even in all the upheaval, than in any other Ottawa hotel.

On May 12, 1984 an Ottawa resident, Fred Walton, asked his wife, Lillian, what she would like as a fiftieth anniversary gift. Would she prefer a diamond ring, a mink coat or a trip? Mrs. Walton thought it over and decided she didn't want any of those things. What she would like would be a night at the Château Laurier. After all, the hotel had been built the same year as Mrs. Walton was born. "Other people had come from all over to stay at the Château, and so would we. We made our reservations for the Gold Key wing and had dinner in the Château Grill. We danced to the music of Moxey Whitney, who played all our old familiar songs." [7]

Fred and Lillian Walton toasting their 50th wedding anniversary in the Canadian Grill, May 12, 1984.

Mrs. Walton also remembered a dinner she and her husband had attended at the Château fifty years previously, in 1934. The Swift Canadian Packing Co., where Mr. Walton then worked, had held a dinner for their staff and salesmen.

Mrs. Marjorie Garden, recognized earlier as one of the original employees of the Château Laurier, gave a CBC radio talk about Christmas in days gone by during the early eighties. By this time Mrs. Garden's eyesight had failed, and she was a resident at St. Patrick's Home in Ottawa. When Jacques Favre heard about Mrs. Garden, he decided to invite her, along with a friend, to spend Christmas 1983 at the Château. Mrs. Garden described that special Christmas:

> "We arrived on Christmas Eve afternoon and were no sooner in our rooms when the management sent up a beautiful basket of fruit. We had a suite of two bedrooms and a sitting room When we went to the Canadian Grill for dinner, the waiter was most attentive and asked if I would like turkey.

'Oh, goodness no,' I replied, 'We have turkey regularly at St. Patrick's Home. I would like some roast beef.' They brought me the most delicious plate of rare roast beef I have ever eaten.

Santa Claus appeared bearing gifts and my friend said the decorations were beautiful. We stayed overnight and enjoyed a lovely, leisurely breakfast on Christmas morning. After that my friend drove me back to my residence. I had a thoroughly good time." [8]

Phase One is Completed

Champagne and caviar were served to the Press on the morning of June 27, 1985. The first phase of the Château restoration was complete. Construction hoardings, which for months had encased the hotel, were removed at noon to reveal the porte-cochere, the new main entry which replaced the old front porch. Mayor Marion Dewar described it as magnificent. "I didn't know they could deliver the level of elegance they have," she remarked to General Manager Denis Beaulieu, who supervised all the restoration from its beginning in 1983. [9] The porte-cochere, a sheltered drive-through with valet service, was

Phase one of the hotel's restoration programme showing the new main entry.

given a glass roof emblazoned with brass lights. Many of the original porch stones were reused in the new structure.

Inside, from the magnificent gold-trimmed ceiling to the re-polished travertine floor, massive columns and stripped oak walls, none of the grandeur had been lost. Gone, however, was the frayed seating area where travellers once waited for airport transportation. Gone also were the stuffed animal heads from 1912. The old chandeliers were replaced by contemporary recessed lighting, and a new black marble front desk was installed on the west wall. A spacious new lounge, set on two levels, was located between the lobby and the area being prepared for Zoé's, the new cocktail lounge and restaurant. The next phase when completed, ushered in a new era for hotel guests.

A New Style

In 1985, a three-tiered price range was introduced for guests at the Château, an approach still in effect at the time of writing. First class, formerly Gold Key, became Entrée Gold. For the top corporate executives who like pampering and all the perks, there are thirty-five Entrée Gold rooms on the fourth floor. This section has its own concierge desk, its own locked entrance to ensure that no other guests go noisily through the halls. King-size beds, sitting rooms and meeting rooms are decorated in rose and green. Continental breakfasts are served in a private dining and reading lounge. In the evening, cocktails and canapés are complimentary. With telephones in the bathrooms, bathrobes, shoe-shine and limousine service, nothing is left to chance.

Business class became the Silver Entrée. The forty-five rooms on the sixth floor are decorated in soft pink or blue. Perrier water is found by the bedside, sheets are turned down at bedtime, and there is a private lounge for breakfast and cocktails in the evening. Economy class became the Premier Entrée. Designed for regular tourists and travellers, these comfortable rooms are those on the first, second, third and parts of the fourth and fifth floors.

On some floors, walls were knocked down to expand the size of rooms to include sitting rooms. All twin beds were replaced by king, queen or two double beds, in response to public demand. The hotel, which once had 550 rooms, now has just under 400.

For A 'New' Hotel, A New Manager

The last few years had not been the best for the Château. The ongoing construction, a decline in government and business travel, general spending cuts and the tough competition from other downtown hotels, had had a negative impact on profits. In 1986 Mr. Peter Howard became the new General Manager, coming to Ottawa from C.N.'s new L'Hotel in Toronto, where he had been General Manager. Oxford educated, Mr. Howard began his career at London, England's Dorchester Hotel in the 1950's. His international experience in major hotels took him from Europe to the Americas, including the Caribbean.

Peter Howard, Château general manager.

Among the 'Howard' innovations in October of 1986, he invited over 340 women to meet Samuel Twining of Twinings' Tea Company in England and to taste some of the firm's products. The *Citizen* reported:

"Twining, a descendant of the 300-year-old company's founder, with his wife Anne, was introduced to guests as they arrived at Zoé's. Everyone was offered a choice of four different teas. Lady Sheila Day, wife of Britain's High Commissioner to Canada, discovered that she and Anne Twining both like to start the day with the same blend of tea.

Among other guests were Aline Chrétien, Eveline Coupal, Carol Towe, Grete Hale, Joyce Loeb, Di Kirkwood, Eve Hyndman and Charlotte Gray." [10]

Media Memories

The Château means different things to different people. William C. Heine, retired Editor-in-Chief of *The London Free Press* and resident of London, Ontario, recalled a visit that George Schultz, then U.S. Secretary of State, made to Ottawa some years ago:

"A dozen or so Canadian journalists and broadcasters were invited to an interview at the Château Laurier at 7 a.m. Most questions were relatively short. Schultz answered them briefly or at length as the subject warranted. One well-known TV personality then asked a long question which grew into a speech, rambling on so long that it was soon evident he was more interested in impressing Schultz with his knowledge than in finding out what Schultz thought. Ending with a questioning note in his voice, the broadcaster waited expectantly. Schultz paused a few seconds, his poker face composed as usual, then quietly said, 'No', and looked around the room for the next question. End of that broadcaster's questioning." [11]

Doug Small, Global Television Ottawa Bureau Chief, has memories of a different sort:

"I recall going to an Iranian rug auction in that room just off the lobby (the old Convention Hall), of becoming separated from my wife, Brenda, trying desperately (and unsuccessfully) to reach her before she bid (successfully) on a Persian rug we couldn't afford. I remember celebrating my daughter Stephanie's thirteenth birthday in the Grill (Brenda and my youngest daughter being in Florida at the time). I remember dancing with her (a lady at last) between courses. I remember the birthday cake that was brought out for her while we were on the dance floor, and the band playing 'Happy Birthday.' I remember the bill — $100.12 for two. And my daughter, of course, didn't drink." [12]

The dreaded announcement by C.N. President Ron Lawless in February 1987, which said that C.N. was looking for a buyer for the Château Laurier, and perhaps its whole hotel group, brought dismay to the Château staff and to the City of Ottawa. Since a proposed sale to Canadian Pacific Hotels had fallen through, and as C.N. wished to get out of the hotel business, the Château would be up for sale to anyone.

Staff and citizens alike were worried about jobs and about the possibility of our own 'all-Canadian' hotel perhaps being sold to an owner from another country. The search for a buyer went on for some time.

Seventy-Fifth Birthday Party

Château staff were determined not to allow the possibility of a sale to dampen their enthusiasm for the proposed seventy-fifth birthday party in June. The first announcement about this festive event was the Château Challenge, a just-for-

These members of the 1987 staff entertained retired staffers at a pensioners' luncheon, accompanied by piano stylist Eddy Prophète, (back row center).

fun contest with serious prizes. Sponsored by *The Citizen*, Air Canada and the hotel, the contest was open to everyone with interesting photos or memorabilia. Judges would determine the three best entries according to their historical interest or value. Objects selected would be displayed as part of the Château's exhibition from June 3 to September 10 and then returned to their owners.

First prize was a week for two in an Entrée Gold Suite in any C.N. hotel, plus two Air Canada tickets to that destination. Second prize was a week for two in an Entrée Gold suite at L'Hotel in Toronto, plus dinner for two at Top of Toronto in the C.N. Tower on one evening of choice. Third prize was a weekend for two in the Presidential Suite at the Château Laurier. All prizes included continental breakfasts.

It was surprising what Ottawa people brought into the hotel. There were menus, photos, ashtrays, vases of glass and silver, and most startling of all, a Sevres china vase with matching Sevres china candlesticks. First prize was won by Carl Fox, a born collector. His amazing sixty-piece collection began when he first spotted an enormous painting of the Château Laurier. Dave McIntosh took second prize for a 1911 Château Laurier brochure he had discovered in a bookstore a few years ago. For a dollar fifty Mrs. Ethel Hamilton had acquired at a church bazaar, a photo of Prime Minister Mackenzie King, King George VI, Queen Elizabeth and Governor General Lord Tweedsmuir engaged in animated conversation while dining at the Château Laurier. She received third prize.

Among the items loaned for the exhibition was a 1942 menu which had been kept as a treasured souvenir. After lunching with his wife and four friends at the Château, a young recruit had hopped a train to the east coast and then proceeded overseas. The menu had been kept as a memento of what they feared would be their last lunch together. All six survived the war.

Many Château employees, at the time of their retirement, had been with the hotel for forty years or more. Management felt they deserved to be honoured on this birthday occasion, so the pensioners were invited to a special luncheon in June 1987. Mr. Dan Oberlander, President of C.N. Hotels; Jean Le Blanc, Vice-President, Human Resources; Claude Sauvé, Vice President, Eastern Region; and Peter Howard, General Manager all joined the celebrations. After the luncheon, a group of present-day employees entertained the guests accompanied on the piano by Eddy Prophète, pianist in Zoé's Restaurant.

These employees photographed in 1982 have enjoyed a long career of service with the Château Laurier. From the left, front row: J.C. Côte*, bellman, 35 yrs.; W.J. Villeneuve*, bellman, 40 yrs.; S.L. Lalonde, room service, 41 yrs.; M.D. Simard, engineering, 36 yrs.; G.J. Belisle*, Auberge, 38 yrs.; J.L. St. Pierre, barman - C.B.R.T., 40 yrs.; N.J. Chénier*, Cock & Lion, 30 yrs.; and Y.M. Prevost, swimming pool, 32 yrs. Centre row: R.J. Desrochers*, bellman, 31 yrs.; J.A. Coulombe, room service, 39 yrs.; L.A. Grouix, room service, 39 yrs.; S.J. Diraimo, engineering, 29 yrsl; R.A. Morin, laundry, 37 yrs.; J.C. Lepage, Cross Keys, 31 yrs. and J.E. Racicot, Cock & Lion, 35 yrs. Back row: R. De Repentigny, bellman, 43 yrs.; G. Bertorelli, chef, 30 yrs.; V. Barresi, chef, 29 yrs.; R.S. Robert, chef, 37 yrs.; E.R. Daviau, engineering, 29 yrs. and L.J. Thérien*, receiving, 35 yrs.
(*Still with hotel at time of publication).

For the pensioners, it was great fun walking about the Quebec Suite and out into the surrounding halls greeting old friends with whom they worked for many years. "It was wonderful to see the girls again," said Noela Miller, a former housekeeper. Lena Lukyniuk agreed. Nicknamed 'the Lucky's', she and her husband, Demetro, had worked in the hotel for over thirty years. Mrs. Lukyniuk was employed in the laundry room where she would iron for eight hours a day. "I like handling clothes. When I see them all nice and folded, that makes me happy. It was my line."

Among the pensioners was Mr. Ciasaglia who had joined the Château in 1934 at age nineteen and worked his way from bus-boy to Banquet Manager. He met his wife at the Château, a young girl who worked briefly in the check room before going to work for the government.

'Through the Years', a retrospective display of photos and mementos, was officially opened to the public during the birthday celebration and remained open at the hotel until September 7. On the afternoon of the party, a town crier stood in the hotel lobby calling out 'Oyez, Oyez' to invite tourists and local inhabitants into the Ballroom to celebrate the Château Laurier's seventy-fifth anniversary.

"If only the walls could talk, what stories they'd have to tell," Environment Minister Tom MacMillan told the crowd who packed the Ballroom for the unveiling of a special plaque.

There has to be a cake at a birthday party, and what a cake it was! The fruitcake contained twenty-one kilograms of butter and sugar, twenty-five kgs. of flour, 21 kgs. of raisins and dried fruit, forty-two lemons and 420 eggs. Ernst Frehner, the hotel's pastry chef, had the task of transforming the cake into a replica of the Château, complete with gabled windows and turrets. "There should be enough cake for 700 people and we have baked a 'back-up' cake in case we run short," the Chef said. Carts of ice cream stood in every corner of the Ballroom with every topping imaginable. Clowns, balloons and the music of the National Press and Allied Workers Jazz Band added to the fun. It was a Very Happy Birthday. [13]

Memories Linger On

The Château continues to hear of guests from the past who love the Château so much, they keep coming back. One recent visitor, Mr. Huntly MacDonald Sinclair, first visited the Château with his father in 1912 as a boy of thirteen. He has stayed at the hotel many times since, and this time he said,

> "Although the reunion of World War I pilots I am attending is being held at another hotel, I couldn't stay anywhere but the Château. (Yes, there are still a few W.W.I veterans around.) I try to get my room overlooking the Rideau Canal." [14]

Mr. Sinclair stayed on at the hotel for a month. He then left for Peterborough to attend a World War II reunion.

Former Mayor, Marion Dewar, enjoyed the events she attended at the Château Laurier in her official role as Mayor, but the memories that are most precious to her are much more personal.

"When I first began to date Ken (husband), we went to the Canadian Grill at the Château quite often. I can recall the charm of the place, and how impressed I was with both the food and the music. Our dates there were always special, and provided the only place we could afford to go and still be 'out on a date.' Our first wedding anniversary was celebrated at the same Grill.

Similarly, I remember being taken by my parents to the Château Laurier pool. At that time, it was one of the few indoor pools in Ottawa open to the public. It was a special occasion for all concerned when we went to that beautiful institution for a swim." [15]

T.C.A. employees, Joan Keogh Rankin (author) and Norah Quinn Bannock, take a poolside break in 1947.

Dave Brown in one of his columns, in the *Citizen*, wrote:

"On a cold day in May 1952, a disillusioned eighteen-year-old Vincent Belle walked into the Château Laurier Hotel. His dream was a job, any job, short term but paying enough to allow him to save to get his freezing backside back to southern Italy.

He had been in the city only two months. They put him to work as a dishwasher and told him he was an apprentice. He finally walked out of the Château Laurier on a Friday afternoon in 1989, with enough money to go any place he wants to. He'll stay here (in Ottawa).

Belle said he was one of the last kitchen-trained chefs to work his way into the upper ranks. 'The way I did it, you had to apprentice three years in each department of the kitchen. There are five departments. It took fifteen years, and then you were a chef de cuisine.' That's about like a kitchen colonel, with the chef being the three-star general." [16]

YOUSUF KARSH

Karsh of Ottawa

YOUSUF KARSH,
KARSH OF OTTAWA

A T THE INVITATION of Myles Craston, C.N. Hotels General Manager in the 1970's, world renowned photographer Yousuf Karsh opened his studio at the Château Laurier in 1973, but his association with the hotel dates from his arrival in Ottawa in 1931.

Mrs. Karsh remarked to the author:

> "We reach out to the world and the world comes to our studio. People arrive constantly from all over the world – personalities to be photographed, many media people to interview Mr. Karsh and museum directors and curators to plan exhibitions and books. We house all our guests at the Château, on the fourth floor in welcoming Entrée Gold suites. Our own personal friends also enjoy Entrée Gold when they come for a visit."

Mr. Karsh has donated copies of each of his twelve books to the hotel for their guests to enjoy during their stay.

In the main floor corridor leading to the Adam Room, there are two glass showcases, one on either side of the hallway. These are for the exclusive use of Karsh for his portraits. People often phone to ask, "Who is displayed in the showcases today?", as these portraits are a contemporary commentary on what is happening in world affairs. For example, among recent Château Laurier guests were delegates from France. To add a French flavour to their visit, Karsh displayed a portrait of President Francois Mitterand and an early photograph of General Charles De Gaulle. When Queen Elizabeth arrives for a Royal visit, portraits of her and the Royal Family are shown.

Fifty-one years ago, the distinguished Canadian, Vincent Massey opened Karsh's first big exhibition of portraits in the old Convention hall (now Zoé's Restaurant) at the Château. People queued up for the event.

When Karsh and his late first wife Solange went to the Grill Room for dinner and dancing in the 1930's, Mr. Helders was the Head Waiter. Karsh spoke of him as a 'splendid man'. The two men became friends and Karsh photographed Mr. Helders. The National Gallery of Canada featured this portrait in its great Retrospective Exhibition, 'Karsh: The Art of the Portrait' in 1988.

Soviet scientist, writer and dissident, Andrei Sakharov, and his wife, Dr. Elena Bonner stayed at the Château and were both photographed by Karsh. Mrs. Karsh gave Sakharov a book to hold during the photo session. It was a beautifully illustrated copy of a recently discovered Grimm's Fairy Tale called *Dear Mili*. Sakharov had time to read it quickly and 'found it to be delightful'.

In 1986 Harry Rasky, the award-winning documentary film maker, made a one-hour-and-ten-minute film of Karsh's work and life, called 'Karsh, The Searching Eye'. It was filmed both inside and outside the Château Laurier. There were beautiful shots of the hotel in sunlight and one of Karsh shaking hands with the doorman. The film was nominated for an Emmy award.

Nelson Mandela, the heroic leader of the African National Congress, and his wife, Winnie, arrived in Ottawa from Paris to stay at the Château, in the summer of 1990. He was quite ill on arrival and cancelled all his appointments except for his sitting with Karsh.

The Most Reverend Desmond M. Tutu, with his wry sense of humour, remarked as he stepped off a plane in Ottawa, "Is this the Ottawa of Karsh?" — a play on words, as the famous photographer is known as Karsh of Ottawa. When told that indeed he was in the right city, His Grace asked if Karsh was in town and if so, might he sit for a portrait. The Lord Archbishop of Capetown and Metropolitan of South Africa was captured on film, and that portrait is shown in this book.

The internationally known Canadian rock star and composer, Bryan Adams, created a sensation at Zoé's when Mrs. Karsh took him to lunch after his sitting. Adams and Mr. Karsh were to meet again in Ottawa in October of 1990 when they shared the joy of their membership in the Order of Canada O.C., Yousef Karsh as Companion.

Mr. Karsh, also enjoyed photographing the three members of the Canadian rock group, Rush, in the Château Ball Room, for a record cover. They sent Mr. Karsh a replica of their album 'Grace Under Pressure,' when it went platinum.

Many young students find their way to Karsh's door. Teachers phone to ask if Karsh will speak to their class. Often the students sit on the floor in the hall outside the studio when there are too many of them to crowd inside, and master and pupils have a happy time.

Both Karsh and his wife, Estrellita, feel the Château Laurier is well on its way back to its former elegance. Their studio is an integral part of the Château life. They have the warmest relations with Mr. Peter Howard, the General Manager and their extended family — the Château staff.

When the Château celebrated its seventy-fifth anniversary on June 3, 1987, Mr. Karsh was among the dignitaries on the platform. He proudly opened the 'Through The Years' exhibit of photographs from the Canadian National Railways files, as well as others from the Public Archives of Canada, the City of Ottawa Archives and private collections.

Yousuf Karsh looks forward to many more happy and productive years at the Château Laurier.[17]

H.R.H. Queen Elizabeth II and Prince Philip, 1984.

Poet and Socialite Duncan Campbell Scott photographed in 1933.

Prime Minister the Rt. Hon. Pierre Elliott Trudeau, 1968.

Andrei Sakharov and Dr. Elena Bonner, 1989.

Bishop Desmond Tutu, 1984.

Nelson Mandela, 1990.

Carrie Fisher, 1979.

Bryan Adams, 1989.

"Rush" 1984. L to R. Alex Lifeson, Neil Peart, Geddy Lee.

Looking To The Future

Innovations in the late eighties at the Château included events such as a Cabaret in Zoé's, with host, Bob Knapp and featuring the Vocal Trio of Dick Maloney, Laurie Nelson and Debra Brousseau, and the music of the Jean-Pierre Allain Trio. On one occasion Cole Porter's music was celebrated, and on another evening the Gershwin years were in the spotlight.

With the coming of the nineties, dancing to the live music of the Norbet Boyce Trio in the Château Grill remained as a Friday and Saturday evening feature. At brunch on Sundays in the Grill, classical music contributes to the tradition established in earlier days.

Afternoon tea has become a daily event at Zoé's. The English tea served with Devonshire cream, scones, finger sandwiches and assorted pastries has given new meaning to 'meet me at the Chateau'. A variety of special events continue to focus attention on the hotel. The tradition of balls, banquets and business remain — only the names change.

Gracious living is emphasized in the multi-million dollar renovations.

The Château Laurier was sold in August 1989, and much to the relief of staff and patrons, it remained in Canadian hands, as the new owners are Canadian Pacific Hotels. Mr. Peter Howard has remained as General Manager of the Château and, in keeping with the actions of his predecessors, has charted an imaginative course for the future. Plans are set to maintain the Château Laurier as both a quality hotel and an exceptional Ottawa landmark. A second multi-million dollar renovation will position the Château for the 21st century. With a new glassed-in terrace overlooking the Parliament Buildings, an expanded boutique mall, a direct access to the impressive new museum of contemporary photography and continuing sensitive attention to the heritage of the hotel, Hay's vision will remain centrepiece for Ottawan and tourist alike. Yes, the 'old lady' is as gracious as ever.

The Château Laurier has a new lustre. The hotel, by combining grandeur with heritage, has been brought full circle to the legacy of excellence left to it by that astute businessman Charles Melville Hays and by Sir Wilfrid Laurier, who gave the Château his blessing.

MY REMEMBRANCES
1943-1952

P*EOPLE ASK* why I am writing about the Château Laurier Hotel. First of all, I have had a love affair with the Château Laurier ever since my Dad took our family to the Château Cafeteria for hot chocolate and muffins one cold and snowy November day after a Remembrance Day ceremony on Parliament Hill.

Later, when I was lucky enough to be offered a job with Trans Canada Air Lines in 1943, I leapt at the chance, as I was bored stiff with the job I was doing in an insurance company. It was a treat just to walk into such an elegant building, but to be there every day, to wander in the lobby, and to see how life goes on in one of the world's finest hotels, was a joy.

For years I have wanted to write about the Château Laurier, but, with moving on an average of every two years with my army officer husband into and out of every military establishment between Montreal and Camp Shilo, Manitoba, I just didn't get at it. Of course, from the fact that we brought up four children as well, readers can guess I've had a busy life.

These closing reminiscences are my personal impressions over the years 1943 until 1952, when I left T.C.A. to be married, and moved to Montreal. Because I worked shifts, I saw the hotel during the day when people rushed in and out on business. I saw it at noon when hundreds of civil servants kept the two revolving doors spinning, on their way to lunch in the Cafeteria or the Canadian Grill. I saw the Château sparkle in the evening and become quiet after midnight.

In 1943 the T.C.A. office was a crowded, noisy place. Telephones rang constantly. A teletype machine clacked and clanged twenty-four hours a day. It carried messages back and forth between our office and our Central Control reservations office in Toronto. The work was exciting. My fellow workers, mostly women in wartime, came from all over Canada. We were a dedicated but wacky group, the kind of people who liked change and excitement.

The Hon. C.D. Howe was in the Château just about every day. As Minister of Transport, Mr. Howe was also the boss of T.C.A. Sometimes he had business with our District Manager, Reg Campbell. No matter what the occasion, he always had a cheery hello for all of us as he walked into the inner office.

One really sweet man, also with the Department of Transport, was Major Robert Dobbs, an older man, a bachelor, who lived in the Château. I would call him a gentleman and a gentle man. Everyone in our office loved him. I think he was lonely sometimes in the evening. He would come to the counter just to talk if we weren't busy, but would never think of doing so otherwise.

At times we would have a particular man come to the office in the evening looking for a young woman to go out with. Whenever we saw him coming, we

Joan Keogh Rankin at work in T.C.A.'s Château office, 1944.

would hide in the back of the office; then, if a passenger came along, we would have to go out. The hanger-on was a real pest.

T.C.A. executives were a friendly bunch. In the beginning this was a small company and everyone knew everybody else from coast to coast. H.J. Symington, the President, was a businessman of high repute. A modest man, he never threw his weight around. W.F. (Bill) English, the Vice-President, was a big teddy-bear of a man, with ruddy cheeks, grey hair and a hearty laugh. He came to the office at least once a month. He would walk in unexpectedly, have a private discussion with Mr. Campbell, then come out and chat with the staff for ages. I think he found out more about our operation in this informal way than if he spoke to us as a group. He was always open to suggestions of how to improve certain procedures or change any aspect of our work, and would encourage us to speak up. If he found someone's idea feasible, he would give the O.K. to make the change.

Other well-known Canadian pioneers in the aviation industry were company department heads. There was D.R. MacLaren, Barney Rawson, 'Tuddy' Tudhope, S.S. Stevens, Ron George, Walter Fowler, Herb Seagrim, Jack Dyment, Al Edwards, Gordon Haslett, George Lothian, Romeo Vachon, Frank Young and Dave Tennant. The only women executives then were the Stewardess Training Programme instructors, all of whom were Registered Nurses.

I remember seeing three great men of the forties and fifties. One was Prime Minister Winston Churchill, walking in the foyer of the Château, a huge cigar in his mouth and his hand raised in the V-for-Victory salute. General Eisenhower strode through the lobby after a reception in his honour, the famous big grin lighting his face. General Charles De Gaulle, ramrod straight in his uniform, was the guest of honour at another reception. The parents of one of the girls in the office had an invitation to this reception which they couldn't use, so she and another friend went to the party. They shook hands with De Gaulle in the receiving line, then proceeded to get giggly on the generous amount of liquid refreshment being served.

Two men who travelled with us a great deal during the war were the Addison brothers, Jack and Harry. Both were large men who smoked big cigars and had quite jolly personalities. They owned Addison Industries and manufactured Walkie-Talkies. They often paid excess baggage charges on the heavy equipment they carried.

Frank 'Budge' Crawley, of Crawley Films, Ottawa, carried large reels of film in big tin canisters, also putting his luggage into the excess category. Max

Freedman, Ottawa correspondent for the *Manchester Guardian*, was a quiet and delightful man. He always had so many books in his arms that he could scarcely carry them. He, too, was charged for excess weight.

One of the wartime 'dollar-a-year' men, F.M. Ross, a lumber executive from Vancouver and later Lt. Governor of British Columbia, sent a bushel of fresh holly from Vancouver to our office each Christmas. Everyone took home a few sprigs. Roy Geddes, a senior administrator in the Wartime Prices and Trade Board, was unfailingly courteous. When I left to be married, he was kind enough to remember me with a gift.

Many of our passengers were engaged in wartime work of some kind. It was a heady feeling to know we were serving in the war effort by expediting their trips and doing what we could to make things easier for those travelling on T.C.A.

The only drawback to the all-night shift was that you were usually finished all your work by 3 a.m., with nothing more to do until 6 a.m. when you started making wake-up calls to passengers on early flights. I used to write letters or read a book. Occasionally, Toronto would send an urgent message on the teletype and if I had dozed off over my book, I would soon be awakened by the bell on the machine clanging.

On no two consecutive days was work ever the same. One day I might work at the Château and make out tickets for people travelling the following day. The second day I could be sent to the airport to work my shift. There I would take passengers tickets or issue them if they didn't have one, check their names on the manifest and weigh their baggage. After announcing the flight departure I would follow the passengers on board. It was my job to count to make sure the correct number of people were there. If all was fine, I told the stewardess that the passengers were all accounted for, then would step back out on the ramp, close and lock the passenger door, walk down the steps and wave to the pilot.

Passenger agents did all those things in the forties and early fifties. That variety made our work so much more interesting than a nine-to-five office job. At the airport, I would be the only woman on duty among a group of male baggage and cargo handlers, mechanics and the weatherman. If we weren't busy, they were sure to play some practical joke on me.

T.C.A. pilots did not take it kindly if we allowed a passenger to go to the airport if such a person was obviously drunk. I would suggest to a person so affected, in a nice way, that it would be better if he (I can't remember a she) would please go and have something to eat and a rest, then I would do my best to get him on a later flight. Some people would protest, but most took it good-naturedly and would wait. If I came across a bellicose character who became belligerent, I would call the house detective, Mr. Stockfish, or the on-duty Bell Captain to deal with the individual.

During the war, all our passenger agents met a great many people. We were often invited to have dinner in the Canadian Grill, if we could get off duty. We were allowed one hour at dinner time, hardly enough time to enjoy the meal. However, if another agent would fill in at the office for us, we had two hours to dine and perhaps have a dance or two. We repaid these favours by working overtime for one another.

An excerpt from the Ottawa Page of T.C.A.'s company magazine *Between Ourselves*, provides a flavour of the times:

> "Never a dull moment here — this will give you an idea of the manner in which the web of intrigue weaves its way around the staff at the Château. Let's look in on some of the girls and their activities in the Capital City during the past couple of weeks.
>
> Baron Silvercruys saying a very elaborate good-bye to all the girls (he was recently appointed Belgian Ambassador to the United States). Colonel Timoshenko of the Soviet Embassy, inviting Norah Quinn and Enid Foster to attend a special preview of some U.S.S.R. films. Lola Gibson and Joan Keogh out hiking with Rifki Zorlu of the Turkish Legation. Lorna McKinnon seen in the Château Cafeteria lunching with George Taraschenko of the Polish Legation. The Count de Hautecloque, newly appointed French Ambassador to Canada, just arrived in Ottawa with his Countess and their EIGHT charming daughters, Woe is us!
>
> Our own Joanne McKay, now Mrs. Raoul De F. Jenner, former Counter Clerk at the Château, will be appearing in *Canadian Magazines* very shortly as the Woodbury Bride. We are certainly thrilled that one of OUR girls was chosen for this exciting assignment."

Ottawa, before the war, had been very short of unmarried young men. The figures were supposed to be around thirteen women to one man. The war changed all that to a surplus of men, and Ottawa women enjoyed having an opportunity to go dancing. However, one thing we all tried to avoid, at all costs, was being stepped on by a serviceman wearing boots with a horseshoe-shaped piece of metal on the soles of his shoes. Your foot would almost be crushed.

I was working for T.C.A. when the Count de Marigny was accused of murdering his father-in-law, Sir Harry Oakes, in the Bahamas. However, he was acquitted at his trial and was later to visit Ottawa and stay at the Château.

About 1950, when emigration from Europe to Canada was becoming common, I had a flight arrive about noon one Sunday when I was on duty alone. It was a wet and foggy day, but with just enough visibility for the plane to land at Uplands Airport. Among the passengers sent to the Château for alternate transportation were two families from Greece who did not speak English. The airport agent had phoned Toronto to advise their relatives of the delay. I phoned upstairs to the Greek Ambassador's residence to ask if he or his son would interpret for me, but they weren't home. By then it was around 2 p.m. I realized that the two women, in their late thirties, with husbands about the same age, three young children and an elderly lady, were likely hungry. The only restaurant open on Sunday in the Château was the Main Dining Room, so I motioned to them to follow me there. When I explained the situation to the Head Waiter, he welcomed them warmly and seated them at the big table in the centre of the room. All the other luncheon guests had already left. Big bowls of steaming soup were soon produced, and I left the families to the care of the three waiters who were serving them and clowning it up a bit to amuse the children.

Later, when I returned, they were all smiles except for the elderly lady who seemed restless and upset. The younger women were trying to tell me something, but I didn't understand. Suddenly it dawned on me that she might need the washroom. I took her by the arm and guided her across the corridor to the ladies' room. A big smile broke out on her face when we walked in. After she had freshened up, she gave my hand a squeeze and we smiled at each other.

Luckily, two or three hours later the fog cleared at Toronto and these weary travellers were on their way to a new life in Canada. I sometimes wondered how they got along.

Another agent, Lola Gibson Ross, and I were on duty one day when a roughly dressed man, looking a bit the worse for wear, came up and spoke to her. He said he had a large amount of money with him and asked if he could leave it with her overnight, as he was going out of town and didn't want to lose it. The agent asked the accountant if she could put the money in the office safe. He agreed, gave the man a receipt and deposited the money in our safe. Next day the stranger returned, looking scruffier than the day before, and with an obvious hangover. He asked for the money and Lola asked for the receipt.

"Well, I'll have to sit down," said the visitor, "because the receipt is in my sock." He removed his shoe and a very smelly sock from which he pulled a tattered piece of paper. He had been involved in a brawl on his wanderings the night before and had spent the balance of the night in jail.[1]

Each morning when our accountant came into the office he took the cash receipts from the day before, tallied them all up, put the money into a cloth bag with the bank book, then handed it to one of us to take to the bank. I often walked nonchalantly down Rideau Street to the Bank of Commerce, carrying several thousand dollars in that bag, in plain view of everyone. None of us ever thought of being robbed and we never were.

One day a man came in and made a long and involved reservation to several cities in South America, with stop-overs for several days in each one of them. I had all the space confirmed, made out a very long ticket and had it ready for him to pick up on the date he had set. He didn't come in that day or the next, and when the departure date arrived, he was a 'No-Show.' I always remembered him. About three years later, he showed up again. I asked why he hadn't let me know he wasn't using his other flight. He told me he had been called away and couldn't contact me. I later found out the truth. He had planned the trip to South America to escape capture by the police but they caught up with him before he came for the tickets. He had just been released from prison three years later.

Another time a Yugoslav citizen living in Canada, who spoke only a few words of English, wanted to fly to Yugoslavia for a visit. It was a Communist country and I was afraid he wouldn't be allowed to return to Canada. I phoned the Yugoslav Embassy and asked the woman on the phone if she would translate for me. She spoke to the man, then told me what he wanted. He went on his flight and about two months later I saw him in the lobby. He gave me a wave and a big smile. Everything must have gone well.

Just after the war, a good-looking army Captain wearing the uniform of New Zealand came to the desk and chatted with me for awhile. He asked if I would like to go out with him when my shift ended. I said, "I don't think so, as I don't know you." "Just a minute," he said, and he disappeared into Peacock Alley. A few minutes later he came back with a lady about his own age, her husband and two girls about eight and ten years of age. He introduced them to me as his sister, brother-in-law and two nieces. Then his sister said, "This is my brother, whose home is in Auckland, New Zealand. He is stationed in Germany with the War Crimes Commission and is here visiting us." Then, amid much laughter, they invited me to go to their cottage the next day for dinner. During the next two weeks, I saw a great deal of that family. The New Zealander flew back to Germany and I never saw him again.

Movie stars almost too numerous to mention have stayed at the Château. A few, not mentioned earlier in the text of this book, who caused a flutter among the young women in our office, were Randolph Scott, Walter Pidgeon, Raymond Massey and Nelson Eddy. Some of the talented and glamorous female stars were Greer Garson, Bette Davis, Marlene Dietrich, Anna Nagle and Helen Hayes.

Paul Anka was an Ottawa boy, and while he was still a young teenager, my brother-in-law, Clay Kingsbury, hired Paul and two other young lads to sing at an Ottawa Board of Trade party. They were each paid five dollars for the evening. As a successful entertainer, Anka returned to the Château a few years ago to record a television special for a U.S. network.[2]

One morning when I came off the night shift, I bumped into a friend newly arrived from Toronto. He suggested we have breakfast together. When we entered the Main Dining Room, we spotted broadcaster and actor, Lorne Greene, seated by himself, and my friend who knew Greene, asked him to join us.

The Hon. Paul Martin remembered a morning when he was walking into the Château and Lorne Greene was coming out of the hotel. "Good-bye, Mr. Martin," said Greene, "I'm off to Hollywood to make my fortune" (little did he know).[3]

Former world heavyweight boxing champ Jack Dempsey, came to the counter and talked to me one night. He had been in Ottawa to referee a wrestling match and was waiting in the lobby for his 12:30 a.m. flight. Jack Sharkey, another ex pro fighter of note, also came to Ottawa several times to referee matches. Each time he came to the counter, he would show me pictures of his family. He was obviously proud of them.

I remember an ambassador, who resided at the Château temporarily, inviting some of our staff to dinner at the Seigneury Club in Montebello, Quebec, about an hour's drive from Ottawa. Several cars were needed to carry us and I happened to ride in the ambassador's big Cadillac with three or four others. It was a very scary drive, as the ambassador drove so fast we were all terrified. I asked him to slow down, but he simply laughed and passed everything on the road. Normally I wouldn't have said anything, but fright made me bold and I informed our host that I would not be driving back to Ottawa in his car. We were all rather shaken.

Once inside, with a cosy fire to warm us and a drink to relax us, we did enjoy our dinner at the famous club where some of us had never been before. The women in our party convinced the men from the office who were there to drive back with the ambassador while we drove home in the other cars.

A few days later, while walking along Sparks Street in my lunch hour, I met the ambassador who greeted me by taking my hand and kissing it. A streetcar full of people was stopped right beside where we were standing, and all the passengers were gawking out the window at the sight of this well-dressed older man kissing the hand of a young woman in the middle of staid old Ottawa, in broad daylight. I blushed and took off quickly.

A friend of mine, an army officer, stopped at the counter one day in 1948 to say hello to me. He introduced me to another officer who was with him, Bill Rankin. Then they went off for lunch in the Cafeteria.

A few days later, Bill came back and invited me to go to a party with him the next week at the Officers' Mess. Four years later we were married. That was thirty-eight years ago, thirty-eight years of a happy and stimulating life together.

People often refer to the Château Laurier as the 'Grande Dame of Rideau Street, or the old lady'. To me, the Château is more like its namesake, Sir Wilfrid Laurier — dignified and hospitable.

Waiter Gaston Belisle delights author with his Canadian Grill recollections.

NOTES

Chapter 1

1. *The Montreal Standard*, Dec. 18, 1909.
2. G.R. Stevens, *A History of the Canadian National Railways*, *MacMillan Publishers, 1973*.
3. *Canadian Annual Review*, 1907, National Archives of Canada.
4. Madge Macbeth, Saturday Supplement to the *Citizen*, 'Château Laurier Begins', Sept. 12, 1953.
5. Madge Macbeth, *Ottawa Citizen* 'Amazing Case of Château Laurier', Sept 19, 1953
6. Macbeth, Sept. 12, 1953.
7. Macbeth, 1953.
8. Jacques LaChapelle, *Architectural Record*. Vol. XXIV, No. 4, 'Architectural Ethics — The Case of the Ottawa Terminals Station and Hotel', p. 293, October, 1908 (Royal Architectural Institute of Canada).
9. *Construction Magazine*, May, 1908 N.A.C.
10. Meredith's letter, *Construction Magazine*, July, 1908, N.A.C.
11. Royal Architectural Institute of Canada.
12. Contracts for Building the Château Laurier.
    a. Record Group 30, Vol. 12634, Items 711 N.A.C. *The George A. Fuller Co. Ltd.*, 949 Broadway, New York, N.Y. A contract between the above and the Ottawa Terminals Railway Co. dated Nov. 24, 1909 for the construction of the Château Laurier Hotel, Ottawa, Ontario and the Union Station.
    b. Record Group 30, Vol. 12634, Item 712 N.A.C., a second contract between the *George A. Fuller Co. Ltd.* of New York and the Ottawa Terminals Railway Co., covering the erection of a Terrace over the tracks of the C.P.R. and the Hull Electric Railway, at the Château Laurier.
    c. Record Group 30, Vol. 12613, Item 441 N.A.C., Aug. 30, 1909, a contract between *Peter Lyall and Sons* and the Ottawa Terminals Railway Company, covering construction of the new railway station at Ottawa and an agreement dated Aug. 3, 1909, between *Mr. James Ballantyne* and the Ottawa Terminals Railway Co. covering installation of plumbing and steam fitting in the new baggage-annex building at the Central Union Passenger Station.
    d. Group 30, Vol. 12613, Item 440, N.A.C. dated Aug. 30, 1909. An agreement between the *Dominion Bridge Co.*, Montreal and the Ottawa Terminals Railway Co. covering furnishing and erection of structural steel for the hotel and station at Ottawa.
    e. Record Group 30, Vol. 12673, Item 1347. N.A.C. An agreement dated May 14, 1910 between *Bishop Construction Co. Ltd.* and Ottawa Terminals Railway Co. covering construction of pipe tunnel, trenches and sewers from the Château Laurier to the Central Union Passenger Station.
    f. Group 30, Vol. 12644, Item 888. N.A.C. An agreement between the *Garth Co. of Montreal* and the Ottawa Terminals Railway Co. for (1) plumbing; (2) brine piping and coils; (3) steam fitting, heating and ventilating; and (4) mail chutes and boxes required in the construction of the Château Laurier hotel.
    g. Record Group 30, Vol. 12673, Item 1331 N.A.C. An agreement between Mr. *Samuel Rosenthal* and the Ottawa Terminals Railway Company, dated Sept. 28, 1911, covering taxi-cab service in the City of Ottawa.
    h. Record Group 30, Vol. 12638, Item 763. N.A.C. Agreement between *Smith Marble and Construction Company Ltd.*, and the Ottawa Terminals Railway Company, covering marble work to stairs and lavatories at the Château Laurier Hotel.
13. Hays' prophesy of disaster paraphased from: Geoffrey Marcus, *The Maiden Voyage*, 'Revelry By Night' p. 113., Viking Press, 1969.

Chapter 2

1. Mrs. Marjorie Garden, former Château executive secretary, now deceased, in correspondence and interviews with author, 1985.
2. Emile Labranche, Waiter, interview with author, 1987.
3. *Ottawa Free Press*, July 23, 1912.
4. Invitations of Duncan Campbell Scott and his wife, Belle Botsford Scott, Rare Book Section, National Archives of Canada.
5. Barbara Williams, Carp, Ontario, interview with author re her father, Jack Ballard, long-time chief engineer at the Château Laurier, 1985.
6. Gratton O'Leary, *Recollections of People, Press and Politics*, Macmillan of Canada, 1977, p. 1977.

Chapter 3

1. Interview with Gordon Sims during Winterlude celebration, *Ottawa Citizen*, 1984.
2. Letter to Mr. Angus Gordon from Rex Beach, American novelist, *Canadian National Railways Magazine*, 1923.
3. Musical Programme courtesy of Château Laurier.
4. Danny Lupino, retired Head Waiter, interview in Ottawa with author, 1987.
5. Edith Lancaster, retired Sales Representative, interview with author, 1984, 1985, 1986.
6. Gordon Oliver, CBO files, Château Laurier.
7. CBO files.
8. CBO files.

Chapter 4

1. Bill Kehoe, CBO, Ottawa, as told to the author, 1987.
2. Merrill Denison, 'The Complete Hotel', *Canadian National Magazine*, July, 1929.

3. Robert Goyette, retired Waiter, interview with author in Vanier, Ont., March, 1985.
4. Tony Popyck, retired Waiter, telephone interview with author, 1987.
5. Tony Popyck.
6. Bruce West, 'Cafeteria Salute', *Globe and Mail* June 20, 1963.
7. Based on information from E.C. Russell, *Fifty Years of Rotary in Ottawa*, 1966; and Russell, *A History of the Rotary Club in Ottawa: 1961-1981*.
8. Merrill Denison.
9. Edith Lancaster, retired Sales Representative.
10. Edna L. Inglis, 'The Magician Behind the Scene', *Canadian National Magazine*, Oct., 1931.

Chapter 5

1. R.H. Ayre, 'With Sled, Skate and Ski', *Canadian National Magazine*. March, 1930, p.5.
2. R.H. Ayre, p.44.
3. Bennett Papers, National Archives of Canada File No. 373277-98.
4. Bennett Papers, National Archives of Canada. File No. 557766-67.
5. Ernest Watkins, *R.B. Bennett: A Biography*. Secker and Warburg, London, Eng., 1963, p. 108.
6. Ross Tolmie, Q.C., in conversation with author, 1987.
7. Edith Lancaster, retired Sales Representative.
8. Henri Seguin, retired Château Laurier Bellman, in conversation with author, 1985.
9. Henri Seguin.
10. G.R. Stevens, *History of Canadian National Railways*, MacMillan Publishers, 1973.

Chapter 6

1. Edith Lancaster, retired Sales Representative.
2. Danny Lupino, retired Head Waiter.
3. 'Housing the Empire's Statesmen', *Canadian National Magazine*, August, 1932.
4. *The Evening Citizen*, Friday, July 22, 1932.
5. Paraphrased from *The Evening Citizen*.
6. *The Evening Citizen*.
7. Edith Lancaster.
8. Château Laurier files.

Chapter 7

1. Edith Lancaster, retired Sales Representative.
2. Edith Lancaster.
3. McKenzie Porter, 'The Toughest Hotel Job in Canada', *Macleans Magazine*, June 15, 1954.
4. Ozzie Williams, letter to author, Feb. 4, 1985.
5. McKenzie Porter.
6. Sylvia Margosches Haltrecht, interview with author in Ottawa, 1990.
7. Steve Phillips, Waiter, interview with author, 1985.

8. Emile Labranche, retired Waiter, interview with author, Feb. and March, 1985.
9. Robert Goyette, retired Waiter, interview with author in Vanier, March 1985.
10. Doris Moulds, Assistant Housekeeper, interview with author in Ottawa, 1985.
11. McKenzie Porter.
12. Duncan Dunbar, *Brotherhood of the Railway, Transport and General Workers: Brotherhood Biography*, Château Laurier files.
13. Edith Lancaster.
14. Allen Noblston, 'Proudly does Monsieur Tassé hone and strop his razors'; *Toronto Evening Telegram*, April 1, 1939.
15. George Tassé, interview with author in Ottawa, 1985 re his father, Paul Emile (Red) Tassé, Head Barber.
16. McKenzie Porter.

Chapter 8

1. Marcel Provencher, former Assistant Night Manager, interview with author in Ottawa, 1987.
2. Robert McKeown, 'The Fabulous Château', *Montreal Standard*, 1946.
3. Dorothy Pearson Baldwin, Kingston, Ont., letter to author.
4. Austin Cross, *Ottawa Citizen*, 1943.
5. Austin Cross.
6. Doug Small, Ottawa Bureau Chief, Global Television, interview with author in his Ottawa office.
7. Prime Minister Mackenzie King, P.M.'s papers, National Archives of Canada.
8. Robert Bryce, retired Deputy Minister of Finance, interview with author in Ottawa.
9. Mart Kenney, letter to author from his home in B.C.
10. Robert Goyette, retired Waiter.
11. Edith Lancaster, retired Sales Representative.
12 Charles Wright, CBO Manager, CBO files.

Chapter 9

1. Lester B. Pearson, *Memoirs Vol. I*, U of T Press.
2. Steve Phillips, retired Waiter.
3. Robert Goyette, retired Waiter.
4. Marcel Provencher, retired Assistant Night Manager, interview with author, 1985.
5. Austin Cross, *The Ottawa Citizen*, 1943.
6. Robert Bryce, retired Deputy Minister of Finance, interview with author in Ottawa.
7. Stanley Knowles, interview with author in his office at Parliament Hill.
8. Hon. Paul Martin, interview with author in his home in Windsor, 1985.
9. Joseph Schull, *The Great Scot: A Biography of Donald Gordon*. McGill-Queen's University Press, Montreal, 1979.
10. Joseph Schull, *The Great Scot*.
11. Charles Lynch, Southam News Service, interview with author in his Ottawa office.
12. George Tassé.

Chapter 10

1. Robert F. Hyndman, Ottawa artist, from letters to the author.
2. Marcel Provencher, retired Asistant Night Manager.
3. Danny Lupino, retired Head Waiter.
4. Edith Lancaster, retired Sales Representative.
5. Austin Cross, *Ottawa Citizen*, 1951.
6. Mrs. Mary Monteith, interview with author at her home in Stratford, Ontario.
7. Cmdr. W.G. Hillaby, Ottawa, Ontario, from letter to author, June 30, 1987.
8. Jack Cahill, *John Turner: The Long Run*. McClelland and Stewart, 1984.
9. Senator Keith Davey, interview with author in the Château Grill Room, 1989.
10. Russell Bannock, retired President of De Havilland Aircraft interview with author at his home in Toronto, 1986.
11. Château Laurier files.
12. Marcel Provencher, retired Assistant Night Manager.
13. Château Laurier files.
14. Patrick Watson, Chairman, CBC, letter to author, Sept. 13, 1989.

Chapter 11

1. Bill Luxton, retired Broadcaster, CJOH, Ottawa, letter to author, July, 1989.
2. Len Weeks, retired Orchestra Leader, interview with author at Ottawa Civic Hospital, September, 1984.
3. Senator Keith Davey, interview with author in the Grill Room at the Château Laurier, May, 1989.
4. Château Laurier files.
5. Charles Lynch.
6. *Ottawa Citizen*, January, 1963.
7. Château Laurier files.
8. C.N.R. Hotel files.
9. Eddie Baxter, in conversation with author.
10. *Ottawa Citizen*, April 21, 1965.
11 Angelo Casagrande, retired Chef, interview with author, 1986.
12. Bill Luxton.
13. Gaston Belisle, Waiter, interview with author in The Grill, May, 1989.
14. Biaggio Tarddio, Waiter, conversation with author in The Grill, May, 1989.
15. Ronald Albert, Waiter, in conversation with the author in The Grill, May, 1989.
16. W. Gordon Foster, former Manager, interview with author at the Château Laurier, 1987.
17. Henri Seguin, retired Bellman.
18. Patrick Watson, correspondence with author, Sept. 13, 1989.
19. *Ottawa Citizen*, October, 1970.
20. L. (Butch) St.Pierre, Bartender and Rep. Local 30 Union of Railway and Transport and General Workers, interview with author, 1985.

21. Miss Myrtle Tostowaryk, retired Executive Housekeeper, in conversation and correspondence with author, 1984, 1985, 1986, 1989.
22. Moxie Whitney, shortly before his death, in a telephone conversation with B.L. Penhale, Publisher, 1989.
23. *Ottawa Citizen*, December 10, 1971.
24. Paraphrased from the *Ottawa Citizen*, April 11, 1971.
25. C.N. Hotel files.

Chapter 12

1. Bernie Gillis, retired Grill Room Manager, interview with author, May, 1989.
2. Bernie Gillis.
3. Marcel Provencher, retired Assistant Night Manager.
4. Mike Duffy, former CBC Parliamentary Correspondent, telephone conversation with author, 1984.
5. Jacques Favre, Executive Assistant Manager, interview with author in his office at the Château, 1983.
6. Rick Brennan, 'Vincent Boileau — Head Barber', *Ottawa Citizen*, April 12, 1984.
7. The late Mrs. Lillian Walton, letter to author, February 2 and 15, 1985.
8. Marjorie Garden.
9. Château Laurier files.
10. *Ottawa Citizen*, October, 1986.
11. William C. Heine, retired Editor-inChief, *London Free Press,* London, Ontario, letter to author, Feb. 24, 1989.
12. Doug Small, Ottawa Bureau Chief, Global Television, letter to author, January 7, 1984.
13. Seventy-Fifth Birthday Party, June 3, 1987, Château Laurier files.
14. *Ottawa Citizen*, Special Supplement, May 30, 1987.
15. Marion Dewar, former Mayor of Ottawa, letter to author, December 6, 1989.
16. Dave Brown, 'Brown's Beat', *Ottawa Citizen*, 1989.
17. Yousuf and Estrellita Karsh of Ottawa, telephone conversation with the author, September 18 and 20, 1990.

Epilogue

All stories not otherwise noted are the author's personal experiences while working for Trans Canada Air Lines at an office in the Château Laurier Hotel lobby from July 12, 1943 until April 20, 1952.

1. Lola Gibson Ross of Victoria, B.C. as told to author.
2. J. Clayton Kingsbury of Ottawa, as told to author.
3. Hon. Paul Martin, interview with author, 1985.

Photo Credits

INDEX